# THINK LIKE AN ELITE RECRUITER

## Master the Questions, Scripts, and Systems to Protect Your Time and Truly Serve Clients and Candidates

# TODD DAWSON

Seshat Press
211 Pauline Drive #513
York, PA 17402
www.seshatpress.com
Send questions to: support@seshatpress.com

Paperback ISBN: 978-1-971288-02-4
ebook ISBN: 978-1-971288-03-1
Library of Congress Control Number: 2026907241


Printed in the United States of America

*For my family, you are my Why!*

*And for the recruiting professionals that realize it's about the candidates and companies we serve selflessly, because what we do is virtuous and contributes to the betterment of everyone we touch.*

# Contents

# Introduction

To be successful as a recruiter demands more than just casual interest. It requires conviction, and it will test your mental toughness daily.

This is why this book is so important to your development. Whether you're a brand-new recruiter, a few years in, or looking to break through to the next level of success, this book will provide the hand-to-hand combat knowledge you need to withstand the crucible of this profession and become truly elite.

My own journey into this business wasn't driven by any natural desire to recruit. It was born from sheer necessity and the realization that my life needed to change dramatically. This was back in the mid-eighties, when technology was virtually nonexistent and standard recruitment practices were in constant flux. I call this period *the covered wagon days*. I was married with two young sons, Matt and Michael (the third, Marcus, didn't come along until some months later), and I was juggling umpiring softball and refereeing basketball six nights a week, just trying to keep the wolf from the door.

In the summer of 1985, I was determined to take my family on a vacation, but all I had was $200. I cobbled together three days of cheap entertainment that included the zoo, the movies, and a small park. That was it. I needed to earn more money, and I knew that recruitment offered no top-end in salary because it provided the opportunity to earn commission. When I met a guy at a recruitment firm with his new car and horrible communications skills—someone who, frankly, I believed wasn't smart enough to carry my lunch pail—who was succeeding wildly, the realization hit me: If he could make it, I certainly could.

I was done living paycheck to paycheck and worrying constantly about the cost of diapers and amoxicillin. I made the leap to recruitment, completely committed to the outcome.

That commitment was tested almost immediately. After I had been on the desk for just a few months, already putting some placements together, my previous employer called me up. They offered me a promotion—a supervisory insurance investigator role in Chicago—and a $10,000 raise.

I promptly declined their offer.

They'd had their opportunity to give me a raise and promote me while I was working for them and, in my opinion, doing a fine job. Since they failed to do that, I told them I was doing great and not to bother me again. In issuing that refusal, I essentially "burned the ships" like Cortez. There was *no* turning back.

Recruitment had been around for a long time, but the executive search profession was still fairly young. When I first became a recruiter, it was wild. Many employers didn't even know that they were the ones responsible for paying the fee. You had to be an absolute expert in everything, mastering the language of the industry, figuring out how to sell, networking with people, and building connections. It was like learning how to start and run a startup business where you were the only employee.

Today, things are more structured, but the fundamentals haven't changed. Technology such as LinkedIn, AI, and Databases are powerful assets because they increase the availability of information, but they don't replace the necessity of talking to people and building trust. The bedrock of success remains exactly what it was when I started: relentless planning, iron discipline, efficient execution, and overwhelming effort.

These fundamentals turned me into one of the highest billers in the United States at the time, culminating in winning the Account Executive of the Decade award from the largest recruiting firm at the time in the U.S., Management Recruiters International (MRI). I was recognized by over five thousand other recruiters to land that honor. Eventually I became the owner of a highly successful, national recruitment firm, helping scores of recruiters develop their own stellar careers.

But there was more than just hard work at play. The essence of what I did, and the philosophy that guided my daily activities, was simple:

*It's not about you.*

We are here to serve. Our purpose is to solve the client's problem by matching great people with great employers, helping the candidate fulfill their hopes, dreams, and desires, and providing talent acquisition solutions to businesses. If you adopt this guiding principle, you will build a career of tremendous success and integrity.

This book will show you exactly how to accomplish that.

# Chapter 1

# Company Orientation – Know Your Onions

If being a recruiter isn't about you, it's even less about the company you work for.

Trust me, your clients and candidates have enough on their plate without having to hear you bang on about how big your firm is, how many recruiters it has, and how many awards it's won.

Does that mean your company's history and size are unimportant?

Not at all. The details of your recruitment firm are actually fundamental to your ability to become a world-class recruiter. It's just unlikely to be something you'll often spend any time talking about.

Yes, if an employer wants to fill a role in a hurry and you know your company has an average "time to fill" of just three weeks, this is information you should know off the top of your head and be ready to share. The tracked performance of your company can be really helpful in establishing authority. But the bare facts about your firm—such as how it got its name, where and when it started, how many placements it makes per year—are far more important to you than to your customers.

This is the true relevance of your employer's details. It's about having pride and satisfaction in the company you work for and feeling like you're part of a successful, exciting team. It's hard—almost impossible—to work long hours with enthusiasm and focus if you don't know what your firm stands for and what it's trying to achieve.

At my company, WorldBridge Partners, when we take on a new recruiter, my son and I provide an orientation process to get them up to speed. We go through a full overview of the firm, including how it got started, and how we grew it to nineteen offices across the company, with almost one hundred recruiters, covering twenty-five or so industries, from aerospace, to legal, to financial services, to manufacturing.

Our clients and candidates might not particularly care about those details, but we certainly do. And we expect our recruiters to care as well. We've built something we're really proud of, and we want our team to feel that they're contributing to the continuation of something special.

And, of course, in that very rare instance when someone does ask one of our recruiters about the history or size of the firm, it's crucial the recruiter is able to reel off some relevant facts and sound like they know what they're talking about. Generally, when someone asks a question along these lines, it's because they want to be reassured that they're working with an established, successful firm that is going to get the job done. In which case, the age of the firm, the number of offices, and the number of recruiters will usually be sufficient.

I hope your employer has provided this kind of orientation already. If not, you can likely find much of this information on the company's website. Read it. Absorb it. Memorize it. And be ready to share it on the off chance that someone asks.

If the website doesn't have much information, speak to your immediate manager and ask them where you can find these details. If they don't know, be bold and contact the owner. Tell them you'd like to know more about the history of the firm, just in case anyone asks about it. This is not a terrible way to show that you have initiative and that you're the kind of person who is going to be taking their work as a recruiter very seriously.

It's very easy to skip this step precisely because it so rarely comes up. I want you to have the following mindset:

*It's not about me, it's about the opportunities I can bring to a candidate and the employers I can help fill roles.*

But, alongside this attitude, I also want you to be detail-oriented and take every small win you can that will ultimately increase your chances of placing a candidate or winning a role. If you're speaking to a potentially major client with multiple roles that need filling, and they casually ask, "Tell me a bit about your firm. How long have you guys been around?" you'd better have a really great answer.

You'd better know your onions.

# Chapter 2

# Familiarize Yourself With Your Database

There are four crucial components or pillars for training a new recruiter:

1. Learning the industry
2. Learning how to recruit (obviously)
3. Learning how to act as a career consultant
4. Learning how to use your database effectively

"But, Todd, the database is just a piece of software—is it really that important?"

My answer is: "100 percent, yes!"

Effective use of your company's database is going to make or break your recruitment career. I'm not exaggerating. Show me a recruiter who underestimates the value of the amazing tool they have at their fingertips, and I'll show you a recruiter who is wasting opportunities right, left, and center.

You actually don't know how blessed you are. In the early days of my recruitment career we kept track of clients and candidates on honest-to-goodness five-by-seven cards that we had to fill in by hand. But I wouldn't swap what we have now. Databases are lightyears beyond those days because they not only store key information about our clients, they also track our progress, send us reminders, and auto-complete routine tasks. And that's before we get into the area of AI and some of the incredible features it introduces.

Your database is a vast filing cabinet of information, but it's more than that. It's like having a virtual assistant, looking after that filing cabinet, and helping you to use the contents efficiently.

I hope your recruitment firm has trained you on at least the basics of how to use their database, but don't stop there. If you really want to leap forward as a recruiter, dig deeper into the software and get curious about the different things it can do. Too many recruiters use a database for the basics and never think about investigating the incredible toolset they have at their fingertips. Try searching for the particular database you use in YouTube and look for tutorials on how to use the features. This is going to really open your eyes as to what's possible and available.

Once you've done that, turn your focus to the quality of the data you input. This is another area where recruiters get lazy. Even though it's much quicker to type in information than write it out by hand, some recruiters still fall into the trap of only recording the basics. In reality, a database is only as good as the data you feed it.

We're going to talk a lot in this book about how important it is to ask your clients and candidates an almost endless series of questions to gather every last scrap of information possible. But to benefit from this, you need to be diligent about recording all this information in the database. Document every email, telephone conversation, and in-person meeting. Upload every scrap of information that you can. Because you never know which detail is going to wind up being crucial later on.

Just a couple of words of warning: Don't forget that Equal Employment Opportunity Commission (EEOC) regulations mean there are certain questions you're not allowed to ask people, such as age, religion, and marital status. If candidates volunteer this information, you can record it, but make sure you note that the person gave you this information freely and that you didn't ask them to reveal this. Everything in the database can theoretically be subpoenaed, so cover yourself by getting specific about how you obtained the information.

And, be smart . . . don't ever record any personal observations about a client or candidate that you wouldn't want read aloud in court someday.

If used correctly, your database will become your most trusted ally in your work. But if you go above and beyond and figure out how to use the database to structure your activities, manage your to-do list and whatever new smart features the software provider adds, you're going to accelerate your growth as a recruiter.

Learning how to use your database efficiently is one of the four pillars of being a recruiter for a reason. Overlook it at your peril.

# Chapter 3

# Setting Goals – Stop Hoping and Start Doing

When I started recruiting, I was as green as they come. I'd never worked in a sales position, and almost everything about the job was new to me. And very little of it was easy or fun. So, here's what I did to light a fire under my seat.

At the time, there was a news story going around about a guy rolling through my neighborhood in a pickup truck, looking for children to abduct. So I took a four-by-six-inch picture of my two boys and stuck it next to my phone. Then I played this mental game with myself—if I didn't make *X* number of calls per day, this lunatic kidnapper was going to get one of my kids.

Crazy, right?

But it worked. I knew intellectually it wasn't real, but by pretending it was, I felt compelled to keep picking up the phone and dialing. Day in, day out. It created a habit that became a routine across my entire career.

Ultimately, this was my Why. I was doing this for my kids. To give them a better life. To make sure they had everything they needed to be healthy and happy. It pushed me to do the hard things, or even just the boring things, that other recruiters procrastinated or avoided entirely.

These so-called *recruiters* usually didn't last long.

You're going to need your own Why. You're going to have days when the thought of spending another hour on the phones, leaving voicemails and getting brushed off by gatekeepers, is going to feel like torture. But if you find your motivation, you'll do it anyway.

I've seen more recruiters flame out than I care to tell you about, and you know what the common thread is? They just kinda show up and hope something good happens. They don't have a plan— they have a dream. And in this business, dreams don't pay the bills. You need motivation and you need goals. Something to give you direction and to keep you moving forward, even when you feel like you can't take another step today.

Obviously, the size and shape of your goals are going to vary depending on whether you're a rookie, a few years in, or a grizzled veteran. But since most people reading this book are going to be in the early stages of their career, let's start there.

## Rookie Goals

Sorry to break it to you, but if you hadn't figured it out by now, for newbies, it's all about the grind. It's about building habits and, most importantly, getting comfortable on the phone. That means knowing how to introduce yourself correctly, engaging people in relaxed conversation in a natural manner, knowing how to leave coherent voicemails, and not panicking when someone expresses interest.

Initially, you're going to suck at it. That's fine. That's normal. The only way to get better is to keep going. Your thousandth call is going to be infinitely better than your first call. And your ten-thousandth is going to feel so smooth and relaxed, you'll sound unrecognizable. There's no substitute for experience in this area, so just accept that there's a learning curve; be patient, and keep on with it.

But that's the intangible stuff. To give yourself something specific to shoot for and to measure your progress, make sure you're tracking the following metrics:

- *Call Volume:* How many dials are you making a day?
- *Connect Time:* How many actual people do you speak to and how long do you spend talking to them—not leaving voicemails, but having real conversations?
- *Presentations:* How many candidates are you presenting to clients?

There are more things you can measure—go as deep as you want—but these are the three that will make the biggest difference to your long-term success. The numbers in all three cases should be going up all the time, especially during your first couple of years. If your ascent is stalling, look for specific ways to increase these numbers. Set daily, weekly, and monthly goals, and then challenge yourself to beat them.

Quality might beat quantity. But quality *and* quantity are going to take you places.

## Veteran Goals

I was at an awards banquet with my wife. The men were all tuxedoed up, and the women were in their finest. We were watching one of the women from my office, Gloria, receiving the Account Executive of the Decade award. To put this in perspective, this award was coming from MRI, so she was part of a pool of five thousand recruiters from about twelve hundred offices.

To win this award, she'd had to demonstrate, over a period of ten years, that she was better than every single one of them.

That is some achievement.

As she was leaving the stage, I leaned over to my wife and whispered, "I can do that."

That was in 1990, and I decided on the spot that I was going to do whatever it took to win the same award in ten years' time. I didn't tell anyone about my goal because this wasn't about bragging or seeking validation. It was a personal challenge and would allow me to set the highest possible goal that I knew would motivate me to push harder and work longer than ever before.

For the next decade, I was one of the top ten recruiters of the year, every year. I never won the annual award (my highest placing was third), but it was my consistency that made the difference. At the end of ten years, I was called up to the stage and received the Account Executive of the Decade. I've thrown away boxes of plaques and trophies I've picked up over my forty years in the business, but that single award still hangs on my office wall.

It wasn't just that I had won the award; it was that had I achieved it by determining that I would do it, and then I had made it happen. This award is a constant reminder of what I can do when I set my mind to it.

If you've been a recruiter for at least a few years, can you set a goal of your own? It doesn't have to be as dramatic as Recruiter of the Decade, but you mustn't ever stop setting targets for yourself. To fail to do so is to atrophy and will speed up your progress toward early retirement.

It could be landing your first six-figure commission. It could be increasing the number of key clients you have relationships with.

Maybe you'd get the most drive and satisfaction out of mentoring the next generation of recruiters and helping them reach their targets.

You already know the ropes, so your targets should be about working smarter, not harder, and fine-tuning your strategies to reach higher levels.

Once you've settled on your personal goals, get specific and write them down or type them onto your fancy tablet. This isn't corporate mumbo jumbo; it's the only way to make sure your goals are real targets you're aiming for.

Get specific here. *I want to make a lot of money* is not a goal. *I want to be able to afford to provide my kids with the best education possible* is better. Next, break down that goal into a series of smaller, achievable goals. It could be: *Make fifty dials a day for the next three months,* or: *Land one $50,000 placement this quarter.*

Then you must put those goals somewhere you'll see them *every single day*. It could be on your office desk, your bathroom mirror, or your phone's lock screen. It doesn't matter, as long as it remains front and center of your brain at all times.

Next, track your progress. You might be able to do this in your database, or you might prefer to create your own spreadsheet. The goal here is to be able to see whether you're succeeding or failing and to hold yourself accountable.

Finally, when you hit your goal, celebrate it. Take a day off. Take your spouse for a great meal. Buy yourself a big, new flat-screen TV. Whatever floats your boat.

And then choose a new, even tougher goal.

None of this is going to be easy. Nothing worthwhile ever is. You're going to have bad days when deals fall through at the last minute, and you'll want to throw your phone out of the window. Suck it up. This is all part of the deal of being a recruiter. The lows are low, but that just makes the highs all the higher. Work on your mental toughness. Practice shrugging off defeats by learning from them, and then, push forward.

Look, I can give you all the advice in the world, but it doesn't mean squat if you don't actually do it. So, get off your butt, set some goals, and start crushing it.

# Chapter 4

# The Chicken or the Egg Dilemma

Recruiters crash and burn so often and so early because the training they've been given is inadequate. Some have the idea that people are either naturally suited to recruiting or not, so "chuck 'em in the deep end, and see if they swim."

I reject this idea utterly. Yes, some people have natural talents or a personality that make them more suited to the profession. But the truth is that, with the right training and a lot of hard work and commitment from the individual, anybody can make it in recruitment.

So where do we begin?

Ideally, a 360 recruiter needs a network of clients before they try to convince candidates to sign with them. But it's also tricky to sign a client when you don't have any candidates to dangle in front of them. Some recruitment firms don't require their recruiters to learn every part of recruitment and, instead, divide work among different people. If you're working in this kind of setup, use the guidance in this book to learn how to do your specific part of the job really, really well, and then study the other parts as well. If you plan to have a long and profitable career as a recruiter, and maybe even own your own firm one day, you're eventually going to have to learn how everything works.

The *chicken or egg problem* refers to firms trying to get their wide-eyed, wet-behind-the-ears newbies to learn everything all at once. The recruits spend the morning calling potential client companies, they spend the afternoon calling prospective candidates, and in between, they're trying to learn the basics of sales and the industry they're recruiting in. There is only a tiny, tiny fraction of people who can take on everything at once and not be overwhelmed to the point of insanity. No wonder so many recruiters run for the hills before they've even made a single placement!

My approach is to start with the elements we've discussed in the first few chapters—learning about the complexity of modern recruiting, getting comfortable with the database, understanding how to take job orders, setting goals, and gathering basic facts about the company and the industry they're recruiting in and for—and then focus on recruiting candidates.

The fact is that marketing to hiring authorities is the most difficult and intimidating side of the job. I believe it's unrealistic to ask a brand-new trainee recruiter to pick up the phone and try to convince a VP that they need your services. That takes a level of confidence, sales nuance, and industry knowledge that can take a year or more to develop.

Candidate work is a lot less stressful, and it gives you plenty of practice in getting comfortable with talking to people, whether it's on the phone, on a video call, or in person. I always say that you want people to know you as their friend who just happens to be a recruiter. And developing those relationships with candidates is a great low-pressure way to get started.

There is, of course, a bit more to it than having friendly chats with people. You need to learn how to identify a good candidate, how to understand the key skills and qualifications that employers in your industry are looking for, and how to recognize when a resume is representing a hidden gem. These abilities will develop with time and experience.

Once I'm happy that the basics have been mastered, I begin easing my new recruiter into the art of the phone call. I don't let them get on the phone until I'm convinced they're fluid enough to sound remotely interesting and in control. I work with them on their introduction, their pitch, their voicemail message—everything they need to make a great first impression.

Then comes the most important part of all: questions.

When a recruiter has a solid intro and is able to build a little rapport with a candidate, the next goal is to get the candidate to open up about their hopes, dreams, and desires. You need to know what really makes them tick. The right questions asked at the right time can uncover a flood of valuable information.

Hand-in-hand with this skill is knowing how to listen. You can't listen with half an ear while you're scrolling social media, or thinking about the next call, or even just waiting for your turn to talk. Listen—really listen—to what the person is telling you and the relevance of it. For the first time in these pages, but definitely not the last, I'm going to remind you, recruiters:

*It's not about you!*

It's also about what they're *not* saying. You can hear things in a person's voice that tell you what that person's thinking and what they might be holding back.

I promise you this: The one question you don't think to ask is the one that comes back to haunt you.

As the recruiter gets more comfortable with this work, I introduce the concept of *marketing candidates*. This is where we flip the script and turn a recruiting call into a marketing call.

The candidate isn't looking for a move?

*Okay, so tell me about the last person your company hired: How did it go? Does your company have any roles you're looking to fill now or in the future?*

As we'll discuss in more detail later, this works in the opposite direction. A client prospect may not have a job order, but they might just be the perfect candidate for an entirely different opportunity.

Finally, there are all the nuts and bolts that come with this work:

- Follow-up and communication
- Keeping candidates in the loop, even when there's no news to report
- Being honest and transparent, even when it's tricky or awkward

Recruiting candidates is the easier part of the work, but that doesn't mean it's easy. There's a lot to learn and a lot to master to make a true success of it. But if you start with the basics, focus on building relationships, and never stop asking questions, you will have a great platform to build on. If you're working for a firm that doesn't have a great training regimen and has just thrown you in the deep end, you may not have the luxury of focusing exclusively on recruiting candidates. If you're in this position, do your best with each part of the job, but focus your efforts on candidate recruitment, and measure your progress by how much you're improving in this area.

As you develop in this part of the job, you should naturally see improvements in every other part of your work. Be patient with yourself, set realistic expectations, and do your best not to get overwhelmed.

# Chapter 5

# Taking and Understanding the Job Order the Right Way

One of your firm's new clients has gotten in touch to say they need help filling role. Your boss drops it on your desk and tells you to take the job order. Are you ready for it?

Or maybe you're talking to a candidate who just happens to have an open slot in his department that needs filling ASAP. Again . . . are you ready for it?

Taking a job order for the first time is exciting because it's a huge step toward, potentially, your first placement and your first commission. And, on the surface, it looks easy. Maybe your firm even has a ready-made form to fill out.

But taking a job order isn't a tick-box exercise. It's so much more than that. To understand a job order—I mean *really* understand it—it's not enough to just take down a few notes and think you know what the client wants. You need to dig deep, ask the tough questions, and get a complete picture of what they're looking for.

The simplest way to prepare yourself mentally is to imagine that you're a candidate for the role. What would you want to know about the position and the company? Everything, right?

Below is a list of the subjects you should cover and the related questions you might ask. This isn't an exhaustive list, and you should feel free to adjust them and add to them to make them more relevant to the employer and your specialist industry. If you're using a prepared form and some of these subjects or questions aren't included, add them in or attach a separate piece of paper.

And, as mentioned in the previous chapter, practice active listening: Does the answer given to one question provide a detail that needs exploring further? Is the client being cagey on a particular issue that suggests they're holding something back?

## About the Employer's Company

- Can you provide a brief overview of the company's history and its position in the market?

- What are the company's core values, and how are they reflected in the workplace?

- What are the primary products or services offered by the company?

- What are the biggest challenges and opportunities currently facing the company?

- Has the company received any recent awards or recognition?

- Are there any recent or planned mergers, acquisitions, or significant changes in leadership?

## Required Education

- What is the minimum level of education required for this position—associate's, bachelor's, master's degree?

- Are there any specific degrees or fields of study that are preferred or required?

- Would you consider a candidate with significant experience who lacks the required education?

- Are there any certifications or licenses that are mandatory for this role?

- If a candidate has a degree in a slightly different field, would relevant experience compensate for that?

- Are there any continuing education or professional development opportunities offered or required for this role?

## Necessary Experience

- How many years of relevant experience are required for this position?

- What if I find someone with less or more experience than you ideally desire, would you want me to present that person?

- What specific types of experience are most critical for success in this role?

- Would you consider a candidate with less experience but exceptional skills and potential?

- Are there specific industries or companies that you prefer candidates to have experience with?

- If a candidate has experience in a related field, how transferable would those skills be to this role?

- What are some examples of past experiences that would be a major advantage for a candidate?

- What are the problems or issues that need to be addressed by a candidate you'd be interested in?

## Must-Have Skills

- What are the top three to five skills a candidate must possess to be successful in this role?

- Are there any technical skills or software proficiencies that are essential?

- How will these skills be assessed during the interview process?

- Are there any skills that can be trained on the job, or are you looking for someone who is fully proficient from day one?

- If a candidate is strong in most areas but lacks one key skill, would you be willing to provide training or support?

- Are there any soft skills (e.g., communication, teamwork, problem-solving) that are particularly important for this role?

## The Hiring Process

- Can you walk me through your typical hiring process for this type of position, step by step?

- Who will be involved in the interview process, and what is their role in the decision-making?

- What is the typical timing between interviews?

- How many rounds of interviews can a candidate expect?

- Are there any assessments, tests, or presentations that candidates will need to complete as part of the process?

- What is the typical timeframe from initial interview to offer?

- How does your company handle reference checks and background checks?

- What was the process for the last person you hired (compare this answer to the previous questions about their process)?

- If I present a candidate in the next three days, how long before I get feedback about your interest?

- If you're interested, how long before we schedule an interview?

- Then what happens?

- Then what happens?

- Then what happens? (Slice and dice the hiring process until you know every step and the entire timeline. If the timeline doesn't match up with what the employer stated while taking the job order, this helps determine not only the urgency in filling the position but the cooperation level and seriousness of the employer.)

## When the Position Needs to Be Filled

- What is the deadline by which you need to have this position filled?

- Is there any flexibility in that timeline, or are there critical deadlines that must be met?

- What are the potential consequences for you, the hiring official, or the company of not filling this position by the desired date?

- Are there any specific events or projects that are driving the urgency to fill this role?

- How much is it costing the company to have this position remain unfilled?

- If the ideal candidate isn't available immediately, would you consider someone who needs a few weeks to relocate or transition from their current role?

## Reasons to Take the Position

- What are the top three reasons a candidate should leave their current job to join your company in this role?

- What opportunities are there for growth and advancement within the company?

- What makes your company stand out from its competitors in terms of employee experience?

- Are there any unique aspects of this role that would be particularly appealing to candidates?

- How does this position contribute to the overall mission and goals of the company?

- What kind of impact can the successful candidate expect to make in this role?

## Knockout Factors

- Are there any knockout factors or reasons why you would immediately disqualify a candidate, regardless of their other qualifications?

- Are there specific companies or backgrounds you would want to avoid?

- Are there any gaps in a candidate's employment history that would be of major concern?

- Have you had negative experiences with candidates from certain companies or with specific backgrounds in the past?

- Are there any personality traits or work styles that would be a poor fit for your team?

- Would you be open to considering a candidate who doesn't meet every single requirement if they bring other valuable skills to the table?

- Are you open to relocating a candidate to fill this position?

## Compensation

- What is the salary range for this position?

- Are there bonus or incentive opportunities (if so, how are they structured, when are they paid, and what is the potential payout)?

- What benefits does your company offer, such as health insurance, retirement plans, and paid time off?

- What did the previous person in this role earn, including base salary and any bonuses or incentives?

- Are there opportunities for salary increases or promotions based on performance?

- Does your company offer any unique or unusual benefits that might attract candidates?

## "Be Curious" Questions

- What have you done so far to fill this position?

- Have you interviewed any candidates yet? If so, what did you like and dislike about them? Who were they?

- Are you working with any other recruiters on this position? What has your experience been like with them?

- Are there any internal candidates being considered for this position? What is their status?

- Are you currently interviewing any candidates? If so, where are they with you in the process?

- Have you made any offers to candidates? If so, what happened in that situation?

- Are there any companies you'd like me to target or avoid in my search?

## Situational Questions

Client Question: What's your fee?

Reply:   I'll be happy to discuss our fee after I have a better and complete understanding of what you're looking for in a candidate.

Client Question: When can I expect to see candidates?

Reply:   Once I've taken all the information I need to begin a search, I'll make a plan, including companies you want me to target and companies to avoid, identifying qualified people at those companies, reaching out to them by phone and having a conversation to determine their qualifications, possible motivations to consider a career change at this stage of their lives, determine their track record, compensation if allowed by law, and interest in your opportunity. If there's a fit, I'll contact you with the candidate's background and determine if you're interested in communicating with them. That may take between five and ten business days.

Client Question: Do you have any candidates right now to share with me?

Reply:    Until I have a complete understanding of your position and I'm able to pin down why this is a great opportunity, I can't speak to potential candidates. I won't be able to gauge their interest until I know everything. In recruitment, there's no such thing as low-hanging fruit.

Client Request: We need someone better than the last person in this role.

Reply:    I understand the desire for improvement. What specific shortcomings did you observe in the previous employee's performance, and what measurable differences are you hoping to see in their successor?

Client Comment: We're restructuring the department, so the role is still evolving.

Reply:    Thank you for the update. How will this position contribute to the overall mission and goals of the company? And how will this restructure impact their position?

Client Request: We need someone with excellent communication skills.

Reply:    Got it. Could you describe a situation in which the person in this role would need to leverage exceptional communication abilities, and what a successful outcome would look like?

Client Request: We really want someone who can think outside the box.

Reply:    That's interesting. How would you define this in a candidate?

The hardest part of the conversation is usually about compensation. Discussions around money tend to be ones that new recruiters are uncomfortable with. But you need to get over it. Compensation is going to be one of the primary motivations for candidates to consider a career change, so this subject is absolutely critical. And believe me when I tell you, if a candidate tells you their move isn't about the money . . . yes, it is. It's *always* about the money!

Imagine that you're a candidate and you ask a recruiter a question about, say, what bonuses are offered and when they are paid. The recruiter responds with: *Um, I'm not sure*. Doesn't exactly fill the candidate with confidence, does it?

That's one of your key aims here. Once you start talking to candidates about the role, you need to know everything about it so you can recruit with conviction and certainty.

The other critical part of the job order is the client's hiring process. Who's involved, how many interviews will there be, what are the key decision-makers looking for, and what types of questions will they ask? The more you know about the process, the better you can prepare your candidates and guide them through it.

I know this is a lot to take in, but trust me when I tell you that it's worth it. Being extraordinarily thorough when taking a job order can avoid a lot of headaches further down the line and will make it easier for you to find candidates that the employer will love. It will feel weird initially, asking so many questions. No one likes to feel like they're being interrogated. But keep it relaxed and personable. You're a recruitment professional taking your work seriously and asking lots of questions and it will actually make you look more like an expert in the eyes of the employer.

And if you ever encounter that rare situation where the employer is irritable about the number of questions or is reluctant to answer them, this is a major red flag that this client is either going to be a problem, or this role is going to wind up being one that no candidate wants to even consider.

Remember, taking and understanding the job order in its entirety is important, not only to fill the position, but, more importantly, for you to understand whether you're confident this is a position you can fill. Many times, employers are just kicking the tires to see what talent is available in the marketplace with no intention of hiring, much less interviewing someone. Think of these questions as your defense against your time being wasted. Every question is important when taking a job order, and there's no such thing as digging too deep.

# Chapter 6

# The Compensation Question

Compensation is the point at which everyone feels awkward. It's the elephant in the room, always has been, always will be. You can try to tiptoe around it, offer them coffee, talk about the weather—but sooner or later, the question of money is going to come up. And how you handle that moment, whether you're talking to a candidate or a client, can make or break the whole damn deal.

For a rookie recruiter, the temptation is to dive straight into the dollars and cents. They think that's what everyone cares about most. And while money is certainly a motivator—let's not kid ourselves, we've all got bills to pay—it's rarely the only motivator, and often not even the primary one. But if you dive into salary details before you understand a person's hopes, dreams, and desires, you're putting the cart before the horse.

I always ask my new recruiters: *Do you want people to know you as a recruiter, or as a friend who just happens to be a recruiter?*

That one question turns this on its head. A friend doesn't lead with the price tag. A friend doesn't pester you about your annual bonus or pry into your savings and pension plan. A friend wants to know what's really happening on a personal level. What's making you tick? What's driving you to consider a change? So, when you're talking to a candidate, and they bring up the compensation question early, don't bite. Not yet, anyway.

You've got to be smooth about it. You can say something like:

> *I appreciate your asking, and we will definitely get to that. But before we do, I really want to understand a little bit more about what you're currently doing and what you might be looking for in a new role. What's motivating you to explore other opportunities right now?*

Get them talking about their challenges, their frustrations, and what they wish their current situation looked like. Because once you understand their Why, the compensation question becomes part of a bigger picture. You can then frame the salary conversation in terms of how this new opportunity helps them achieve those deeper motivations.

Now, inevitably, they're going to press you. They'll want to know a range, a ballpark . . . something. And that's okay. You can acknowledge their concern without throwing out a number right away. A good strategy is to turn the question back to them and ask what their current compensation is. In some states you have to be careful with that question because of legal restrictions.

## Legally Speaking: Rephrasing the Salary Question

If you're in a region of the U.S. where asking a candidate about their current salary is not allowed, try some of these alternative questions to get some insights without stepping on any legal landmines:

- Assuming it's offered, what level of compensation do I need to negotiate on your behalf for you to accept a position?

- What would I have to negotiate on your behalf for you to be interested in this opportunity?

- What are your salary expectations for your next role?

Often, when answering these questions, the candidate will voluntarily tell you their current salary so they can justify their response. And, of course, if the information is given to you without you having to ask, then no one can have any complaints. However, when information about their salary is given freely, the statement must be noted as "volunteered" in the notes you enter into your database.

If the candidate is hesitant to share their current pay, you can suggest a broad range:

*My client has indicated they will pay commensurate with experience. So whether you're making $75,000 or $200,000, my client wants to see these candidates.*

Then you can pivot back to the fit:

*Before we get too deep into the compensation details, is this the kind of opportunity that aligns with your career goals and what you're really looking for?*

It's a bit of a dance. You don't want to look like you're withholding or being evasive, but at the same time, you don't want to be distracted from the more important issues. The Candidate Data Sheet is your friend here. If you're meticulously filling this out—and you should be—you'll develop an understanding of not only their current salary, but also their salary expectations for a new role. This all comes, once again, from asking the right questions and digging beyond the surface-level information you find on a typical resume. It's the art of asking questions, buddy. That's what this business is all about.

When you're talking to an employer about a job order, the compensation question is just as crucial, but your approach is slightly different. You need to understand their budget, of course. But more than that, you need to understand their urgency and their expectations for compensation. If they're trying to lowball the salary for a senior-level position that's been open for six months, for example, that's a red flag. You've got to have the guts to push back and say:

> *With all due respect, if the going rate for this role is $100,000, and you're only willing to go up to $80,000, you might be limiting your talent pool.*

The key difference is that, unlike your conversations with candidates, at some point the question about your fee is going to come up. But the strategy is more or less the same. As far as you can, simply avoid talking about compensation until you've fully explored and understood their pain points and the problem they need you to solve.

What kind of talent are they looking for? How critical is this hire to their success? Once you understand the scope of the challenge, only then should you have a conversation about your fee and demonstrate the value you bring to the table. If you were just sending them resumes and the relationship was purely transactional (yes, this is how a lot of inexperienced recruiters operate), then none of this would really matter. But you're different. You're not just shuffling resumes; you're providing a tailored solution. And you're potentially interested in developing a long-term relationship with the employer.

There's also more to the deal than just the salary. Benefits, work-life balance, career growth opportunities, and company culture—all these factors play a significant role for both candidates and employers. Sometimes, for instance, a candidate will take a slightly lower salary for a better opportunity overall, and sometimes an employer will pay a premium for the perfect fit. We'll get into this part of the negotiation in more detail later, but for now the main thing to remember is that the compensation question is only one small part of the equation. So, when candidates and employers try to put this front and center, take control of the conversation and help them see that understanding motivations, building relationships, and finding the right fit for everyone involved is far more important.

It's a delicate maneuver, but master it, and you'll be way ahead of the game.

# Chapter 7

# Familiarize Yourself With Your Candidate Data Sheet

All right. Listen up, because this is where the rubber meets the road for recruiters, especially if you're a rookie. If you want to really understand your candidates and get all the mission-critical data, you need to make the Candidate Data Sheet (CDS) your best friend.

If this sounds obvious, you're right; it is. But here's what happens: Recruiters start out using the CDS religiously because it reminds them what to ask and guides them through the process. But once they've done a dozen, they think they've got it down; they start doing it off the top of their head. It's no mystery. Filling in a form feels like something only a rookie who needs their hand held should have to do. And no one wants to be a rookie for more than five minutes.

Get over it.

Filling in the CDS is not just for beginners. It's not a crutch exclusively for newbies. It's for every recruiter who cares about collecting a full and complete candidate profile so they can maximize the chances of finding them the right role. If you get lazy and start thinking you can manage without it, that's when you'll start missing stuff and the quality of your work will go down. And the whole point here is to improve as a recruiter over time, not get steadily worse because you're "too smart" to fill in a form.

It's also important not to underestimate how powerful this form can be. If it feels to the candidate that you're just asking questions off the top of your head, they may get bored or impatient. But if they know you're completing a form, the process feels more official and the candidate is more likely to accept that this is just something that has to be done.

The front of the CDS is pretty straightforward and mostly covers what is already on their resume. But there will always, always, be something that has been left off. So don't think of this part as duplication. You're being thorough and making sure that you have all the factual details. For example, a candidate's resume doesn't usually outline the reasons they've changed positions over the years. This needs to be explored because the hiring official is certainly going to want to know those answers. Being armed with that information enhances your credibility to the hiring official.

But this is just scratching the surface.

The real gold, the stuff that separates the good recruiters from the great ones, is on the back of the CDS. This is where you dig into what truly makes a candidate tick, what drives them, their true motivation, and whether you can actually help them. And the very first question you'll see staring back at you on that back page is:

*What do you like about your current position?*

This might seem like a basic question, but the answer, and more importantly, the way they answer, tells you a heck of a lot. This is the true power of the CDS. It's not just about extracting key information; it's also a way to subtly encourage the candidate to open up and start giving you the juice. It's not always about what they say, it's about how they say it. Keep your ears open to this. When you hear frustration, a wry laugh, or a weariness in the reply, don't ignore it. This is your cue to ask more questions on this subject and get to the source of this verbal body language. Now the CDS is helping you turn a simple fact-finding interview into a conversation.

Back in my day, we didn't have these fancy data sheets, and instead we had to rely purely on our questioning skills to get this same information. We'd have to probe, listen, and really think on our feet to uncover what made a candidate consider a move. So, while the CDS is a modern convenience, the purpose behind it—understanding motivation—is timeless.

That first question is just the start. You're also going to be asking about what they don't like about their current situation. What are their hopes, dreams, and desires for their career? What's prompted them to even take your call? Are they just kicking the tires, or are they genuinely looking for something better?

What you're doing, aside from developing a relationship and maybe even a friendship with the individual, is nailing down both their personal and professional motivation. What's driving them in their career? What are their long-term goals? And equally important, what have they done to help themselves thus far in reaching those goals? Have they updated their resume? Are they talking to other recruiters? What actions have those recruiters taken? This tells you a huge amount about their level of urgency and how serious they are about making a change.

The CDS is a wonderful tool because, at the end of the day, we're trying to figure out if we can actually help this person. Are their qualifications a fit for the kinds of roles we typically handle? Is their motivation strong enough to see a job search through?

And here's a little bonus for you:

The information you diligently gather on that CDS isn't just for the immediate job you might be discussing. You never know when that candidate, even if they're not a fit for today's opening, might be perfect for something down the line. That thoroughly completed CDS becomes a valuable record, a treasure trove of information you can tap into for future opportunities.

Don't look down on the CDS just because it's a form that's associated with rookie recruiters. Recognize its value and get familiar with it. Know it inside and out. Understand the purpose behind every single question. Practice using it. It's not just a piece of paper—it's your roadmap to understanding candidates and their motivations, and, ultimately, how you can be successful in this business. Treat it with the respect it deserves, and it will pay you back tenfold. It's the foundation upon which you can build a stellar recruiting career.

# Chapter 8

# Assembling a List

I started recruiting in what I jokingly refer to as the *covered wagon days*. My entry into this profession predated many of the technological advancements we now take for granted. In practical terms, this meant relying on five-by-seven index cards and the Yellow Pages to build my initial contacts. Success in that era was heavily dependent on the ability to ask insightful questions and to meticulously identify potential candidates and clients.

LinkedIn has made all of this information much more readily available, allowing for the easy identification of professionals within specific parameters. However, the mere accessibility of data should not be mistaken for a comprehensive understanding of the talent landscape. The true value in assembling a list of candidates and employers lies not just in the quantity of names, but in the quality and strategic depth of those connections. While modern tools make it easy to compile a list, the skill a successful recruiter must acquire is the ability to intelligently expand this network and gather meaningful information about each contact.

This requires a commitment to the art of asking questions.

In my early career, when tasked with a search—for instance, a sales leadership role in a particular city—my approach wasn't to blindly contact everyone with a relevant title. Instead, I would leverage my existing network, reaching out to trusted contacts within the industry to inquire: "Who are the most effective sales leaders you know in this market?" This initial question would then introduce me to new people of whom I would ask the same questions, leading me to even more conversations. This allowed me to rapidly create a meaningful list, all built upon insightful questioning.

This core principle remains as relevant today as it was decades ago. While platforms like LinkedIn provide an excellent starting point for identifying potential contacts, they are merely a gateway. The crucial work lies in the conversations you initiate. During discussions with candidates, go beyond their resume and ask about their respected peers. When engaging with hiring managers, inquire about their competitors' key hires and emerging talent.

Assembling your list is a continuous and dynamic process. It never ends. You never reach a certain number and then put your feet up, job done. The market is constantly moving and so, too, should your list. I developed what I called my *Perpetual Plan*, a system of consistently adding and categorizing contacts by industry, specialization, and location. Through effective questioning, I would also gather valuable intelligence about each individual—their accomplishments, career ambitions, and even their challenges. This proactive approach meant that when a new search arose, I wasn't starting from scratch; instead, I was engaging with a pre-existing network of informed contacts.

## The Perpetual Plan: Building Your Network for Sustained Success

I've championed the Perpetual Plan throughout my career. It's a proactive method for building a rich pool of potential candidates and employers, meticulously organized by geographic locations, professional disciplines, and products or services. It's a strategy that avoids the headache of starting each search from a blank slate and instead lets you harness the power of ongoing information gathering and network expansion.

In short, you're going to transform every interaction into an opportunity to enrich your understanding of the talent landscape.

## Step One: Define Your Niche

Begin by clearly identifying the specific geographic markets and industry sectors on which you will be focusing your recruiting efforts. This targeted approach allows for more focused list building.

## Step Two: Establish a Foundation

Start compiling your initial lists of potential candidates. Leverage professional networking platforms such as LinkedIn, industry-specific associations, and any existing contacts you may have. Don't worry if initial growth is slow. A small, well-curated list is a valuable starting point.

## Step Three: Ask Questions

In every conversation you have—whether with a potential candidate, a hiring manager, or an industry contact—make a conscious effort to ask thoughtful and probing questions. Go beyond surface-level information to understand their expertise, career aspirations, and professional networks.

## Step Four: Actively Solicit Referrals

Make it a routine practice to ask every relevant contact for recommendations of other high-caliber professionals within their field. Inquire whom they respect and who might be a good fit for potential opportunities. Aim to gain multiple referrals from each meaningful conversation.

## Step Five: Create a Robust Documentation System

Maintain a well-organized system for recording all the valuable information you gather. This could involve using a Candidate Data Sheet to capture comprehensive details about each individual, combined with your company's database. Aim to document contact information, skills, career history, accomplishments, and crucially, referral sources.

## Step Six: Categorize for Efficiency

Segment your growing network based on key criteria such as location, job title, industry, and specific skill sets. This will enable you to quickly identify relevant individuals when a new search arises.

## Step Seven: Continuous Growth and Maintenance

The Perpetual Plan is not a one-time task. Make a commitment to regularly add new contacts to your lists and update existing records with any new information you acquire through ongoing conversations and market research. You'll know you've mastered this when virtually every conversation yields new introductions and expands your list.

## Step Eight: Leverage Your Network

When you receive a new job order, your Perpetual Plan database should be your first point of reference. In the early days, this might not always produce anything useful, and you may have to carry out new searches and seek new contacts. But comfort yourself with the knowledge that this project is going to add to your ever-expanding list. Eventually, your database will succeed more often than it fails.

The Perpetual Plan lets you get away from the frustrating process of constantly reinventing the wheel. When you have a deep and comprehensive network, you're ready for virtually any recruiting challenge this industry can throw at you. And at its heart, it's simply about being curious, asking questions, and spotting movement in the market.

For those new to the profession, it's essential to recognize that strategic list assembly is a core competency, not a "nice to have." It requires dedicated effort and a mindset focused on building genuine connections. Your network is not limited to potential candidates—it should also encompass hiring authorities, HR professionals, and influential figures within your target industries. Cultivate the habit of asking your placed candidates for referrals within their organizations and inquire hiring managers about other companies facing similar talent needs.

I don't miss the covered wagon days. Technology doesn't just allow recruiters to operate faster, it also allows them to develop larger and deeper lists. But the underlying principle that determines the efficacy of that list remains constant: a robust and strategically assembled network, cultivated through the consistent practice of asking effective questions.

Commit to this fundamental aspect of the business, and you will lay a solid foundation for a long and prosperous career.

# Chapter 9

# Write and Practice Your Introduction

You've done some research. You've got a name in front of you; you dial their number, fully expecting to get their voicemail . . . but instead the person picks up. What now?

Are you prepared for this moment?

Because I'm sure you don't need me to tell you, you've got approximately three to five seconds to introduce yourself, grab their attention, and convince them to have a conversation with you.

If you're one of those rare-as-rocking-horse-poop, natural salespeople who can get anyone's attention without even trying, you're all set. But if you're one of the 99.99 percent of recruiters who need to learn these skills, this is where you're likely to fumble over your words and come out with something like this:

Sarah: ABC Corp, Sarah speaking.

Newbie Recruiter: Uh . . . hi. Is that Sarah?

Sarah: Yes, it is. Who's calling?

Newbie Recruiter: Oh, hi, Sarah! My name is Todd from . . ." [Long, awkward pause] " . . . from . . . WorldBridge Partners. We, uh . . . we do recruiting.

Sarah: We already have a recruitment firm we use.

Newbie Recruiter: Ah, okay . . . well . . . um . . . I have a candidate you might be interested in. Can I tell you a bit about him? He's pretty good.

Sarah: I don't really have time. Thanks for calling. [hangs up]

Newbie Recruiter: [repeatedly bangs his head on the desk]

That, my friend, is what happens when a recruiter hasn't practiced their introduction, hasn't done their homework, and doesn't understand the value they're bringing. They sound unsure, they don't give the prospect a good reason to take the call, and they ask closed-ended questions that make it easy for the person to just say no and end the call. Sarah has already taken hundreds of calls like this; she's tired of them, and she's well-practiced in just brushing them off.

So, you've got two choices. You can either keep trying, stumbling your way through your intro, and maybe—and that's a big maybe—after a few hundred calls, chance upon something that works. Or, you could take the time to think about your intro, write something down, and then practice it until you can spit it out perfectly, on cue, without even having to think about it.

Have a guess which route I'm going to recommend . . .

Like I said before, don't make the mistake of thinking that you're too smart and too grown-up to work on the basics. New recruiters—especially those without good teachers—think writing something down and practicing it is beneath them. *It's just talking on a phone*, they think. *How hard can it be?* And then, after leaving fifty voicemail messages, someone actually picks up, and they're totally unprepared and ill-equipped to grab someone's attention in the five seconds they have to make something happen.

The reality is that you're going to spend far more time sending emails and leaving voicemails than actually talking to people. You can spend three or four hours a day on the phone and only actually speak to three or four people. You can't afford to waste those opportunities. You need to be ready to deliver your powerful introduction confidently, naturally, and without even having to think about it. Nerves can get the better of the best of us, but if your introduction is so practiced it's instinctual, you'll be able to deliver it, no matter how anxious you feel in the moment.

In this chapter and the next two, we're going to figure out the key parts of your telephone conversations. We're going to write them down and we're going to practice them until you're word perfect. The "pitch" and the "voicemail message" are coming up, but for now we're going to focus on the introduction. The pitch is the most important, but you'll never get the chance to deliver it if your introduction isn't sound. So, this is the right place to begin.

## A Killer Introduction

Imagine you're calling a hiring authority, a VP of Sales at some company, to pitch a candidate. You can't just say, "I've got this guy; he's great. You want him?" That's not going to cut it. You need something more refined, something that grabs their attention, and something gives them a reason to reject their natural reflex, which is to hang up. You need to help them understand WHY they should listen, and you need to do it fast. Something like this:

> *Hi, Fred, this is Todd from WorldBridge Partners. While conducting a search recently for one of your competitors, I came across a candidate who really stood out among their peers. I wanted to take a quick minute to share a little bit about their background with you to see if they might be someone you'd have an interest in.*

This is simple. And maybe it sounds too simple. But let's break it down and understand why this kind of introduction is so effective.

- *Hi, Fred, this is Todd from WorldBridge Partners.*
  First of all, you give the person your name and company without wasting time explaining that you're a recruiter. It's unnecessary. They're going to figure that out in a moment anyway. But before they do you're going to drop your bait.

- *While conducting a search recently for one of your competitors, I came across a candidate who really stood out among their peers.* The word *competitors* is a magic word. It immediately reminds the person that they're in a competitive market and implies that (a) you have inside information that they don't have, and (b) that if they don't listen to you, they might lose out.

- *I wanted to take a quick minute to share a little bit about their background with you to see if they might be someone you'd have an interest in.*
  Now that they're in a position where they're curious and feeling compelled to at least hear you out. You ask them for the tiniest commitment possible: sixty seconds to hear about the candidate.

The whole thing is just fifty-six words. It only takes ten seconds to say. But it has everything needed to give the recipient a reason to have a conversation. It won't work every time—no introduction is perfect for every situation—but it'll work more often than not. And that's infinitely better than winging it and hoping for the best.

You can use this introduction as is (obviously replacing my name and company with your own), or you can tweak it slightly to better fit how you naturally speak. But don't mess with this too much. You need to get to the point, mention that you've been talking to one of their competitors and then ask for sixty seconds of their time.

Once you've written down something you're happy with, it's down to you to practice it. This is nonnegotiable. You need to recite this introduction out loud, again and again. Practice in front of a mirror, practice with a colleague, practice in your car. The goal is to make it sound natural, confident, and conversational—not like you're reading from a script—and then, to reach a point where you can say it in your sleep. That way, when you're nervous, you'll instinctively fall back on what you've practiced. Trust me on this.

## Hooking Candidates

The introduction will be a little different if you're reaching out to a potential candidate, but in many ways this version is a little easier. Most people are flattered when they receive a call from a recruiter and are more likely to give you a little time to make your pitch. The only difference is that I would recommend having two different introductions—one for when the candidate has been found through a referral and one for when you've found them through market research.

> *Hi, Jill, my name is Todd and I'm a recruiter with WorldBridge Partners. I was referred to you by John Smith, who spoke very highly of your skills in sales. I just wanted to take a quick minute to see if you're open to hearing about an interesting opportunity that just came across my desk.*

In this scenario, it's okay to introduce yourself as a recruiter. Why? Because the candidate on the other end will wonder if they're about to be headhunted and be offered a massive pay raise. They're going to give you more leeway on the call than an employer. But if the candidate has been referred to you, it's smart to mention this right out of the gate because this is going to give you credibility and ensure you get their full attention.

If there's no referral, you can simply fall back on a little flattery:

> *Hi, Jill, my name is Todd and I'm a recruiter with WorldBridge Partners. I know you and I have never spoken before, but I wanted to reach out to you personally and confidentially. Do you have a minute? I just have one question for you: If I could show you an opportunity that's better than your current situation, would you be interested in learning more?*

Provoking their curiosity is still going to be your main weapon here, so it's a minor change. The main thing to understand is that, even though candidates are easier to get into conversation than employers, you still want to be respectful of their time. Remember, these passive candidates aren't sitting by the phone waiting for your call. They're busy working. You need to get to the point quickly and offer them something of value.

## Avoid the Trapdoor

One thing to absolutely avoid in your initial introduction is falling into what I call the *pitch trapdoor*. This happens when someone agrees to talk to you and you immediately start spewing out all the details about the candidate or the job in your initial contact. They haven't even said they're interested yet! They'll just sit there and let you talk, extracting all the information they can, and then politely tell you they're not interested, leaving you with nothing.

Hold your horses! Give them just enough to pique their curiosity and invite them to say: *Tell me more.*

I'm not an expert in fishing, but even I know you don't throw the whole tackle box at the fish you're trying to catch. You use a lure to get their attention and then reel them in. Same thing here. Your introduction is your lure, and then you're going to reveal information gradually, so they don't get bored or distracted and swim away. More on this in the next chapter.

So, to sum it up:

- *Know your material:* Understand your candidate or the opportunity inside and out.

- *Write it down:* Craft a concise and compelling introduction that gives the recipient a reason to hear you out.

- *Practice, practice, practice*: Say it out loud until it sounds natural and confident.

- *Keep it brief:* Respect their time and get to the point quickly.

Getting your introduction right is the first crucial step in the recruiting process. It sets the tone for the entire conversation. It can be the difference between landing a great candidate or a new client and a potential candidate hanging up on you. So, take the time, put in the effort, and master this fundamental skill. It'll pay dividends down the road; I guarantee it.

# Chapter 10

# Write and Practice Your Pitch

You've delivered your telephone intro smoothly and confidently, and they've agreed to give you a minute. This is cause for celebration. Any time you get past your introduction without getting hung up on is a win in itself these days. But now comes the part where you've got to deliver something that'll make them want to keep listening.

Something that'll make them think: *Hmm, even though this is usually when I hang up, this recruiter sounds a little different. This might actually be worth my time.*

Now, you hit 'em with your *grabber*. This is where you reveal the juiciest bit of info about the candidate, the key accomplishment or experience that's going to make their ears perk up. It must be concise, and it must be impactful.

For example, if you're marketing a tech sales professional, you might say something like:

*This individual in their last three years consistently exceeded their sales targets by over 30 percent annually, bringing in five multi-million-dollar accounts.*

The key here is specificity and relevance. Tailor that grabber to the kind of hiring authority you're talking to and the types of roles they typically manage. What are their pain points? What kind of talent would really move the needle for their organization? That's what your grabber needs to speak to.

And then—this is crucial—you've got to ask a direct question to gauge their interest. Something like:

> *Does that sound like the kind of professional your team could benefit from?*

or:

> *Does that individual sound like someone you might be interested in learning more about?*

Now, listen closely, because this is where a lot of recruiters undo all their hard work. You've done really well to get to this point, so don't blow it. Once you've asked that question, you *zip it!* Go quiet and give them all the time they need to respond. Don't jump in with more information. Don't feel the need to fill the silence. That pause can be powerful. It gives them a chance to process what you've said and formulate a response.

If they say: *Yeah, tell me more*, that's great! You've got your foot in the door. But this is where you have to be careful not to fall into the trapdoor I mentioned in the previous chapter. Your instinct might be to just unload everything you know about the candidate, but resist that urge. They've indicated that they're interested but you don't yet know exactly how much. They might just be curious, or they might not have a real need for your candidate and they're just trying to extract information.

So, instead of spewing information, you need to qualify the opportunity. You need to find out if they actually have an open position and what they're truly looking for. You can transition to this by saying something like:

> *I'd be happy to share more details about this individual. But before I do, could you tell me, are you currently looking to add someone with this type of background to your team?*

Even if you already have a hunch they might be hiring, asking directly gives you a much clearer picture. If they say yes, then you can start asking those deeper questions about their specific needs, the urgency of the role, and what they've done so far in their search.

Remember, it's easy for them to say yes to keep things going, but the questioning afterward is what separates the good recruiters from the rest of the pack because your follow-ups are not so straightforward. You're going to dig into *why* they're interested. What specifically caught their attention? What are their current challenges? This information is gold, because it allows you to tailor your further presentation of the candidate and truly demonstrate the value you bring. And, of course, it helps you figure out whether this is a real opportunity.

But what if they say no or *Not right now*? Don't just give it up. Every call has value. You may only get a few chances every day to talk to a real person, so milk this opportunity for all its worth. If the candidate isn't of interest to them, flip the call. Ask about other potential needs within their organization. Ask them if they know anyone who might be a good fit for the role you're filling. Ask what their dream opportunity would look like. Because you've internalized the rule that you never, ever, pass up the chance to try to recruit someone.

## The Candidate Pitch

The principles above apply equally to pitching to a candidate. Once you've got their attention, hit them with your grabber, but don't give away too much.

> *I'm working on a role that offers the opportunity to lead a team in developing the sales program for a new database. The company's received heavy investment and they're looking for someone who can significantly increase their impact in this space. Is that something you'd be open to learning a little more about?*

It's the same strategy. Give them the juice, ask them the question, and then wait as long as it takes for a response. If you get a yes, then you don't spill the beans. Instead, pivot to questions that give you more information about the candidate. This helps you determine whether the opportunity you have truly aligns with their needs and aspirations.

> *Great, I'm happy to hear that. Before I dive into the specifics of this opportunity, could you tell me a little bit about what you're looking for in your next career move?*

or:

> *What aspects of your current role are you finding less fulfilling, and what are you hoping to find in a new position?*

You also want to gently inquire about their current situation. You might ask:

> *Have you been actively exploring other opportunities recently?*

or:

> *Are you currently interviewing with any other companies?*

If they indicate that they're not interested in the opportunity you've teased, just as before this is *not* the end of the conversation. Again, you should now flip the call:

> *Okay, I understand this particular role might not be the right fit for you right now. However, I talk to professionals in this industry every day, and I often come across a variety of interesting opportunities. If I were to come across a role that sounds like your dream job, one that really hits all your key criteria, would you want me to reach out to you about it in the future?*

When they say yes, follow up with:

> *Out of curiosity, what would that dream job look like for you?*

Now you can start filling in your CDS.

If they're not interested in any opportunity (maybe they're close to retirement or have just moved into their dream role), don't forget to do some more exploration and see if there's any movement in the market they're aware of that you're not:

> *Although this opportunity isn't quite what you're looking for, you're obviously an expert in the industry, and you might be able to direct me a little. Do you know of anyone in your network who might be a strong fit for a role like the one I just described?*

Notice that I didn't ask if they know anyone *looking*—I asked if they know anyone who might be *qualified*. That's not an accident. If you're asking lots of questions, you're doing great. But the next level is learning how to word those questions just right, so people are more likely to give you a positive response—and the intel you need.

That initial pitch after an employer or candidate has given you their time is critical. It's your chance to grab their attention, pique their interest, and set the stage for a productive conversation. Just like the introduction, write it down and practice it until it rolls off your tongue naturally. And most importantly, learn to control the flow of information. Qualify first, present second, and always be ready to flip the call. That's how you make the most of every single interaction.

# Chapter 11

# Write and Practice Your Voicemail Message

Until you've been a recruiter for more than ten years, and you've got an epic list you can dig into whenever you need it, you're going to be making a lot of outreach calls. And, like it or not, most of that time is going to be spent interacting with voicemails.

This doesn't mean you're doing anything wrong. It's just that people are busy and don't like taking calls from numbers they don't recognize. So it has been, so it always shall be.

It's also not a waste of time to leave a message. Providing, of course, you do so strategically, and don't just record any old blabber in a bored voice that makes it abundantly clear this is the fiftieth voicemail message you've left today. This tends to happen with new recruiters because they rarely, if ever, get a response to their voicemail messages and so they conclude that it's wasted time. Just something to be rattled off as quickly as possible so they can get to the next call. The quality, as a result, is poor, and so it becomes a self-fulfilling prophecy. Fewer and fewer people call back, so the recruiter puts less and less effort into their voicemail messages, and eventually no one calls back.

The secret to a voicemail that inspires action in the recipient is to recognize that your voicemail is not about you, it's about them. What's in it for the person you're trying to reach? High-quality candidates and hiring authorities are busy folks. They've got their own fires to put out. So, when your name pops up, and they don't recognize the number, why should they take the time to listen to your message, let alone call you back?

You need to give them a reason. A good one. And, just like the previous two chapters, to do this effectively, you need to write your presentation down and practice it. This isn't some casual chat with a buddy. This is your chance to make a first impression, and you want to make it count. Think about what you want to say and how you want to say it. Be articulate. Sound like you know what you're talking about. Dare to let a little enthusiasm creep into your voice.

For that initial voicemail, your message should be crisp and to the point. You want to introduce yourself and your specialty:

> *Hi, Mr. Smith, this is Todd, and I'm a recruiter who specializes in placing Business-to-business sales professionals.*

Right off the bat, they know who you are and what you do.

Next, you've got to give them a hook. This is the same principle as speaking to them in person, where you capture their curiosity or use the magic *competitor* word:

> *I'm currently working on an opportunity to head up a new sales division, and you were recommended to me as someone whose career is on the rise and who could be a really good fit.*

Or:

*While conducting a search in your area for one of your competitors, I discovered a sales professional who really stood out among their peers.*

Finally, ask for a return call, leaving your phone number. Keep it concise. Don't ramble. They don't have all day.

If they don't call back—which is perfectly normal even if you get really good at leaving enticing voicemails—that doesn't mean you give up after one try. Persistence with a purpose is key. You're going to make three attempts in total.

For your second attempt, your message can be slightly different. You've already introduced yourself. Now, you might want to reiterate the value you're bringing. Maybe you have some insights about the market in their industry, or perhaps you have another candidate in mind that could be a fit for a different role:

*Hello again, Mr. Smith, this is Todd from WorldBridge Partners. I left a message a few days ago regarding a potential fit for your team. We're seeing some interesting movement in the sales market, and I believe some of the professionals I'm working with may align with your needs down the line. If you'd be so kind as to return my call, I can be reached at 555-314-1592. Thanks again.*

If you still don't hear back, the third message can be a bit more direct but still professional. You might even offer to connect on a different basis, like a quick chat about the market or to see if they know anyone who might be a fit.

*Mr. Smith, this is Todd again. I understand you're busy, but I wanted to make one last attempt. I'm consistently speaking with sales professionals in the industry and wanted to briefly connect to see if there's an opportunity for us to collaborate or if you know of anyone in your network who might be exploring new options. My number is 555-314-1592. I look forward to hearing from you.*

Remember, with each message, you're building a tiny seed of familiarity. You're showing them you're persistent, but not in an annoying way. You're offering potential value. And even if, after three messages, you still don't get a reply, this still doesn't mean you're failing. For all you know, the recipient might have written your number down, intended to call you, and got distracted. Maybe six months down the line they'll be looking for a new hire, or a new role, and they'll find the slip of paper on which they wrote down your details. So much of recruitment is a numbers game. Just keep at it.

You'll get far more chances to hone your voicemail message than your opening introduction to a real person. But you should still practice your delivery before you first get on the phone. Aim to sound confident. To sound like you believe in what you're saying. Don't mumble. Speak clearly, enunciate, and don't go too fast or too slow. If you sound unsure or unprofessional, they're certainly not going to call you back.

Even if it's just through your voice on a recorded message, you can still make your first impression a good one. Practice and practice and practice your scripts out loud until they sound natural, and you don't have to think too hard about the words. And be tenacious in your follow-ups. This isn't a one-and-done exercise. Three is the right number of messages to balance between persistence and annoying the person you're calling. Getting this part right can make all the difference in getting those calls returned and building those crucial relationships.

# Chapter 12

# Daily Structure

A fresh-faced rookie dashes into the office, jittery as a caffeinated squirrel, but ready to conquer the world of executive search. He plants himself down at his desk, full of purpose and intention, and then . . . well, then the chaos begins. Instead of beginning his daily structure, he's like a toddler in a room full of shiny objects.

First things first, the inbox beckons like a siren song. He dives headfirst into the digital abyss and reads every single email, even the ones about discounted office supplies and Brenda's cat's birthday. Then, naturally, he feels the need to respond to each and every one, crafting eloquent prose about matters that have nothing to do with actually placing a candidate. Ten minutes turns into thirty, and he's still busy with emails.

Then, a fleeting thought of actually recruiting crosses his mind. He opens up LinkedIn to hunt down some top talent. However, three clicks later, he's deep into the profile of his college roommate's cousin's dog walker, marveling at their impressive collection of doggie coats. An hour vanishes into the social media ether, leaving him feeling vaguely informed about the canine community but precisely zero steps closer to filling his open job order.

He makes a half-hearted call or two, leaving voicemails that sounds like he's auditioning for a community theatre production—stumbling over his words and forgetting to include his call-back number. Then, feeling like he's accomplished a monumental task, he rewards himself with a deep dive into the office snack drawer.

By lunchtime, our rookie has been in the office for four hours and has effectively mastered the art of bouncing from one unproductive activity to another, leaving a trail of digital crumbs and unreturned phone calls in his wake. No focus, no routine. Just pure, unadulterated inefficiency.

I'm being a little bit mean. No recruiter (we hope) is ever quite on that level of inefficiency. But anyone who has ever worked at a recruitment firm will spot some elements above that they recognize in others . . . and maybe even in themselves.

You're going to be better than that. Because whether you're fresh out of the gate or you've been around the block a few times, if you're just showing up and winging it every day, you're leaving money on the table, plain and simple. You're also probably feeling like you're always chasing your tail and wondering where the day went. That's not the way to build a business.

And make no mistake: This desk of yours is your own darn business.

The first thing you've gotta get your head around is that structure doesn't mean being rigid. It's about being in control. To channel Mr. Miyagi, "If you don't control your day, your day will control you."

Start by creating a schedule for a typical day. Dedicate specific blocks of time to specific activities, when you focus on either calls or follow-ups. Don't mix up the two. Nothing will make you more inefficient and chaotic. You'll lose focus. You'll lose momentum. And you'll find yourself bouncing all over the place. Don't bounce! You need to develop a habit that becomes a routine.

Here's an example of what your day might look like:

- 9 a.m.–11 a.m. *Morning Power Hours:* This is prime time for making initial outreach calls to employers. People are generally getting their day started, and you have a good chance of catching them.

- 11:00 a.m.–12:30 p.m. *Midday Follow-up and Research:* Return calls, send follow-up emails, and conduct research on potential candidates or companies.

- 12:30 p.m.–1:30 p.m. *Lunch:* Don't skip it or eat at your desk. You need fuel to keep going, and you need time away from your screens to rest your eyes and your mind.

- 1:30 p.m.–3:30 p.m. *Afternoon Power Hours:* Another dedicated block for phone calls, primarily for recruiting. This could also be for follow-ups, debriefing candidates after interviews, or marketing calls.

- 3:30 p.m.–5:00 p.m. *End-of-Day Wrap-up and Planning:* Review your day, update your notes, send out fee schedules, and plan your activities for tomorrow. This helps you hit the ground running in the morning.

This is just an example, and you'll need to adjust it based on your specific market, time zone, and the ebbs and flows of your work. But the key is to block out specific times for specific activities and stick to it as much as possible.

Why is this so important? Because it connects your Why with what you do. Go back to your motivations for getting into this business. Do they include helping people find great opportunities and further their career, building a successful career for yourself, providing a great life for your family? When you have a structured day, you can see how your daily actions are contributing to those bigger goals. If you set a target of making forty-five outreach calls during your morning power hours, and you make forty, you feel a sense of accomplishment. You're moving the needle.

And look: There will be days when things don't go according to plan. A client might call with an urgent need. Or a candidate might call with an unexpected question. Some flexibility is needed. But having a solid daily structure allows you to handle those unexpected events without completely derailing your progress. You'll take the unexpected call, deal with it, and then go back to whatever you were doing before without missing a beat or wondering what to do next.

Commit to creating a daily structure that works for you and that allows you to be the most effective and efficient recruiter you can be. It'll make a world of difference to your productivity, your earnings, and your overall satisfaction in this profession. Take control of your time, and you'll take control of your success.

# Chapter 13

# Yes or No? Bracketing

There are few better moments in a recruiter's day than when you manage to connect with a real person, you deliver your pitch as smooth as Captain Picard's head, and you get a "Yes, I'm interested," or words to that effect. Suddenly, you forget all those unanswered calls and endless voicemails, and the effort that you were just moaning about is all worthwhile.

We discussed how to handle a positive response in Chapter Ten, but it never hurts to remind ourselves of the essentials:

- Acknowledge the interest.

- Apply the brakes (don't give away the juice).

- Ask qualifying questions.

- Understand their motivations.

- Complete a job order or CD.

But what if it's a solid no?

Let's face it: Your offers are going to be rejected far more often than they're welcomed. That's just the nature of the beast. They're busy, they're content, they've been bombarded by other recruiters.

There's nothing that's going to magically move them from their "not interested" stance.

This is where a real recruiter earns their stripes. You don't just say: *Okay, thanks, bye* and move on to the next call. That's amateur hour. And I promise this is true . . . the average recruiter just doesn't know how to make the most of this situation and turn it into an overwhelming positive. Remember: You're only going to speak to a handful of people on any given day, so don't waste this opportunity.

When they say no, your first aim is to keep that conversation alive. Find some common ground, talk about sports, ask them about their weekend, ask them about their family. Be a human being. This ability to turn a *failed sales call* into a *friendly conversation* takes practice and will come more naturally to some than others, but it's how you make yourself memorable and set yourself apart from other recruiters.

The first thing you can do is acknowledge their position. If they say they're happy in their current role or don't need any candidates, say something like:

> *That's fantastic to hear! I'm genuinely glad you're in a good spot.*

or:

> *That's fantastic to hear! I'm genuinely glad your team's in good shape.*

Agreeing with their objection takes the wind out of their sails a little bit. It shows you're not just some pushy salesperson.

Then you can engage in a bit of small talk. If you struggle with this, keep a current list of industry-relevant news and ask them for their opinion. Just keep the conversation going.

Next, you gently transition. You might say something like:

> *You know, even though this particular opportunity might not be the right fit for you right now, you're clearly someone with valuable experience in this field. I'm always looking to expand my network of talented professionals. . . .*

See how we're shifting the focus? It's not about the job anymore, it's about them and their connections.

This is where the concept of what I call *bracketing* really comes into play. Bracketing is a strategic way to navigate the *I don't know anybody* response when you ask for referrals. People often default to thinking about whether they know someone who's actively looking for a job. But that's not how it usually works. The best candidates are often passively employed.

So, instead of a direct question like: *Do you know anyone looking for a new job?* which usually gets a no, you bracket the question by focusing on qualifications and your specific needs. You paint a picture of the kind of person you're looking for and ask if anyone comes to mind who might fit that description, regardless of whether this person is currently job hunting.

Think of it like this: You're not asking if they know someone who has their house up for sale. You're asking if they know anyone who lives in a three-bedroom condo with a view of the beach. Except, in your case, you're looking for people with a particular kind of expertise, a certain track record, or experience in a specific area. You're opening the person's mind in a whole new direction, and they'll suddenly discover they know lots of people you would be very interested in meeting.

Here are some examples of bracketing questions you can use after someone says they're not interested in your opportunity:

- *You know, this opportunity involves a strong background in AI engineering. Thinking about your colleagues or past coworkers, does anyone with that kind of experience come to mind?*

- *We're looking for someone who has a proven track record in AI engineering. In your professional circle, who do you know that's particularly strong in that area?*

- *The ideal candidate for this position would have a strong understanding of AI engineering. Who in your network is particularly knowledgeable in that space?*

- *Considering the kind of work you do, are there any professionals in your field whose skills and experience you particularly respect?*

- *Even if they're not actively seeking a change, who are the sharpest people you know in our industry?*

- *You mentioned you've been at Tech Company, Inc. for five years. Over that time, who are some of the most talented individuals you've worked alongside?*

- *Thinking about individuals who have left your company in the past, where did some of the really strong performers end up?*

See how these questions are framed? They don't directly ask if someone is looking, but rather, they focus on qualifications and past associations. This often jogs people's memories. They might not have thought of someone as a potential candidate before, but when you frame the questions around skills and experience, a name might pop up.

If the conversation is going well, keep going. People like to feel like they're viewed as an expert and someone who is well-connected, so play on this. Tell them how helpful it is to speak to someone who knows the industry so well and ask more questions.

Here are a few to get you started:

- *What other AI-focused companies are in your area? Do you know anyone over there?*

- *Which companies/divisions/offices have been performing the best recently?*

- *Who's been increasing their staff/team?*

- *Are there any other managers you know who I could present my candidate to?*

- *Whose products/services are doing really well right now?*

- *Who do you know at XYZ company?*

- *Which companies have had the best performance over the last three years?*

- *Which company hires the best people in your area? Who do you know over there?*

- *Which companies are decreasing their territories?*

- *Who was the best person (doing this type of job) at your previous employer?*

- *Has anyone left your company in the past six months? Where did they go?*

- *Do you have a sister office? Who is your counterpart there? Who is the best professional in that facility/office?*

- *Has your company hired anyone in the past six months? Where did they come from? Who came in second?*

- *Who would you consider to be a leader in your industry/ competition/company?*

- *Who's your biggest competitor (company or person)? Who do you know over there?*

- *Have you heard anything about mergers or acquisitions in your industry?*

- *If your company were looking to hire someone, where would they look? Who would they call?*

- *If your manager were asking you for help filling a position, who would you tell them to call?*

- *Who is someone I should stay away from?*

- *Who is the biggest gossip in your industry—the person who knows everybody and everything?*

- *Are there any new competitors in your area/industry?*

- *Who was your mentor as you were coming up?*

- *Who is the best up-and-coming professional working in your area?*

- *Do you know anyone who has interviewed lately? Where?*

- *Who was the most talented person at your last company?*

- *Who is the most talented person at your current company?*

- *Who do you know that you would love to give a leg up to career-wise?*

- *Are you aware of anyone looking to relocate to this area?*

- *Do you belong to a professional association? Who heads up that association/chapter?*

If you can get useful responses to even just a few of these questions, you'll be amazed at where this can take you. Chances are that you'll get a few company and people names that are new to you and that you can add to your call list. Imagine if every person you spoke to were to give you at least three names of people to reach out to, and each of those people gave you three names, and so on. This is how you end up mapping out an entire industry and building an incredible network of people you have not only pitched to, but also befriended.

These details will also highlight any movements in the marketplace— which companies are hiring, downsizing, or expanding into new territories or industries. This information, if you follow the breadcrumbs, can lead you to a rich vein of new clients and candidates.

But even if you don't get much useful information from the person, you've still had a conversation. You've built a tiny bit of rapport. You've expanded their awareness of you. And before you hang up, you always, always ask that one crucial question with a setup:

> *You know, Mr. Jones, I'm in the market every day. I speak to around a hundred people a week, and I'd hate to share with you in a future conversation about a position I just filled only to have you say you wish I'd called you about it. So, if I were to come across the absolute perfect opportunity for you down the road, that dream job you've always envisioned, that diamond in a coal mine, would you want me to reach out?*

Almost everyone will say yes to that.

And the next time you call, they won't know if you're calling to tout business or because you've actually found their dream job for them. You'd better believe they're going to take your call!

Handling a real person on the phone is about being prepared for both interest and indifference. When they're interested, qualify and proceed cautiously. When they're not, pivot, ask strategic questions, use bracketing to uncover hidden candidates, and always leave the door open for future contact. That's how you turn a no into a potential lead down the line. You're not just trying to fill one job, you're building a network . . . one conversation at a time.

# Chapter 14

# Dive Into Motivation and Cooperation

You've amassed a nice store of experience points, my friend, so it's time for you to level up and add some extra skill points to your Candidate Affinity ability (my grandkids assure me this is correct lingo for people who play video games).

In Chapter Seven, we discussed the importance of the CDS and how to use deeper questions to learn more about the candidate's status and motivations. But there's more to uncover here. When you have a solid, three-dimensional image of your candidate, you're in a prime position to better connect with them and enjoy a better level of cooperation.

This is important because, as every experienced recruiter knows, candidates are like wild horses. They're full of energy and enthusiasm and strength, but they need a firm hand if they're going to gallop to their new role with purpose.

You're the expert here. Yes, the candidate knows a lot more about the specifics of the job they're applying for (maybe). But when it comes to actually impressing an employer and getting a high-quality job offer, you have to be the one to set the pace.

But we're getting ahead of ourselves. First of all, let's remind ourselves why understanding candidate motivations is so important.

If you've filled in the CDS correctly, you'll have all the facts down. The history, the education, the qualifications. But that's just the first layer. The real gold, the stuff that's going to determine whether you can actually help this person and whether they're worth your time, lies in understanding what drives them.

Think about it. You can have a candidate who looks fantastic on paper, hits all the qualifications, but if they're not truly motivated to make a change, you're going to be spinning your wheels. They might go through the motions, ace the interview, but when it comes down to it, they'll stick with their current gig. Why? Because the desire, the need for something different, their true motivation just isn't there.

So, how do we uncover the candidate's true motivations (because, hate to say it, not every candidate will be entirely truthful with you right out of the gate)? The CDS gives you a starting point by prompting you to ask what they like and dislike about their current role. But you can't just take those answers at face value. You have to dig deeper. Ask them *why* they dislike certain aspects. What impact does that have on their day-to-day? What are the unkept promises that might be fueling their desire for a change?

Then you get to the core question: *Why are you considering a new opportunity?*

Their initial answer might be something generic, such as: *Looking for a new challenge* or *Seeking the next step in my career*. That's fine, but it's your job to peel back the layers. What does *next step* actually mean to them? What kind of growth are they looking for? Is it career advancement, skill development, or something else entirely? Remember, there are only so many core motivators—career path, financial improvement, work-life balance, a better company culture or direction. . . . You need to figure out which ones are truly driving this particular candidate.

For instance, if they say their commute is too long, don't just note that. Ask them what they would do with that extra time each week if their commute were shorter. Would they spend more time with family? Hit the gym? Pursue a hobby? That's the *real* motivation behind wanting a shorter commute. Understanding that deeper desire, their Why, allows you to connect with them on a more personal level and to tailor your approach.

Now, we're ready to talk about cooperation. You can find a perfectly motivated candidate, but if they're not willing to work with you, you're going nowhere fast. Motivation and cooperation go hand in hand. Someone who is genuinely motivated to make a change is far more likely to be cooperative. They'll return your calls and emails promptly. They'll be open and honest in their answers. They'll follow through on commitments, such as sending you their resume or showing up for interviews on time.

And nurturing this cooperation always starts with understanding their motivation. If you know why they want a new job, you can frame opportunities in a way that resonates with those drivers. When you present an opportunity, don't just rattle off the job description. Highlight how this new role addresses their specific motivations—the better career path, the potential for increased earnings, the improved work-life balance, and so on.

You also need to set clear expectations and exchange commitments. Right from the start, explain how you work, what you expect from them, and what they can expect from you. If you're going to invest your time in helping them, what are they willing to do in return?

> *Mr. Candidate, if I call you with an opportunity that aligns with what you're looking for, can I count on you to return my call within twenty-four hours?*

Get their buy-in on the process. This isn't being demanding. You're simply establishing a professional partnership built on mutual respect and a shared goal. You're within your rights to do so, and it's in everyone's best interests to have this level of understanding in place.

If the candidate agrees in principle but fails to cooperate in practice, you have an opportunity to identify red flags, nice and early in the process. For example, if a candidate tells you they're desperate to leave their current job but haven't even updated their resume, how motivated are they really? If they consistently fail to return your calls or provide the information you need, that screams a lack of cooperation, which often signals a lack of true motivation. You've only got so much time in the day, and you can't afford to waste it on candidates who aren't serious. As I always say, *we* decide whom we work with, not the other way around.

It's also crucial to understand if there are other people involved in their decision-making process. Have they spoken with their spouse or anyone else who has input into the decision about the possibility of a move? What do their family's needs and desires look like? Failing to ask these questions can lead to deals falling apart at the finish line, wasting everyone's time. A truly motivated candidate who is serious about a change will likely have had these conversations already or be willing to have them.

The art of asking questions is paramount in this business. Don't be afraid to probe, to challenge assumptions, and to really understand what drives your candidates. The more you know about their motivation, the better equipped you are to find them the right opportunities and to ensure their cooperation throughout the recruiting process. It's not just about filling a job or landing that tasty commission. Remember, none of this is really about you. It's about helping candidates to achieve their career aspirations, and finding clients to perfect their team. And when you have that underlying drive, you'll naturally want to uncover those true motivations. Accomplish this, and the cooperation will follow.

# Chapter 15

# The Mental Part of Recruiting Is the Real Challenge

You never forget your first placement. And mine was a doozy.

My client was a great candidate, an Ivy League graduate, and I was trying to place him with an insurance company. Ironically, if I'd been more experienced, I wouldn't have presented him to this employer because he didn't have the right career history. But because he was an Ivy League graduate they were really interested. There's a discussion to be had about whether it's right to send out candidates whose experience isn't a great fit, because they're still smart and look good on paper, but we'll save that for another time. The point here is that I was keen to make my first placement, and I was pushing hard in every direction I could.

The Regional Vice President at the employer really loved my guy and quickly offered him the job. This would have been great news on my own, but it was going to be an $18,000 fee, of which my commission was $9,000. To put this in perspective, this fee was three times the average fee the firm I was at was used to receiving. My first placement, and it was a monster!

But then I hit a snag. I got a call from an HR guy, and they didn't want to pay the fee. They felt that $18,000 was too much and they wanted to negotiate.

At this point, I could have worked out new terms to make sure the deal would go through. It would still be a sizeable fee, my candidate would get the job, and I would set myself up well with the employer for future placements.

Of course, I did none of that. . . .

I dug in my heels. Hard. I told the HR guy in no uncertain terms that we had a deal at $18,000 and that if they didn't pay it, they weren't going to get the candidate.

The HR guy was a bit snippy and said something along the lines of: *You must not want to work with us really bad.*

To which I replied: *Well, maybe you don't want to work with me really bad. But I don't care. You're going to pay the fee, or you're not getting my candidate.*

I think some of the conflict for me was irritation. We had a deal, and now they were trying to negotiate after the fact. And that fat commission that was going to put food on my family's table was going to be threatened. No, no, no. That wasn't going to happen.

So, in the end they paid the $18,000, and my first placement went down in history.

My mentor, Gary Adams, was sitting across from me and had been listening to the conversation. He told me that I'd handled it perfectly. Today, I'm not so sure. I had right on my side, but it wasn't necessarily the most business-savvy move. I could have agreed to a small reduction, allowed the HR guy to save face, and built a good relationship with the client that could have led to further placements.

But what this story does illustrate is that a lot of success in this business takes place between the ears. The one thing I absolutely did right in that situation, as green as I was, was to be mentally tough and fight for my corner. And this grit, determination, and stubbornness served me well over the years, even if over time it was tempered with some business nuance.

It's this kind of strong mental game that you're going to need if you're going to make it long-term in this business. This is what truly separates the recruiters who build careers from the ones who wash out.

I see these fresh faces come into the business all the time, and they simply do not comprehend the sheer difficulty of what lies ahead. We can tell them about the high failure rate—around 70 percent don't make it—but it's like trying to describe the ocean to someone who's only ever seen a puddle. They nod, they smile, and they think: *You've never seen how hard I work*, but the reality of getting kicked in the shins day after day, week after week, when it feels like nothing is ever going to happen . . . it just doesn't register.

I watched a great Netflix series about elite tennis players, and I was amazed at how frequently these phenomenal athletes, with their precision and skill, could lose one set of tennis and mentally give up. That's truly the main difference between the good players and the great players—that mental toughness to stay at a high level and not be discouraged when things get rough. Rafael Nadal was a master at this. He played every point as if it was the first and only point of the entire match. Nothing before it, and nothing after it. His intensity never dipped.

It's the same in recruiting. The endless phone call sessions and email messages are the back-and-forth rally of your day. Sometimes the ball is going to clip the top of the net, and whether it lands on your side or the opponent's is out of your control. But your mental fortitude is what ultimately wins you the match. It's only when you can accept the setbacks, put them behind you, and push forward without fear of failure that you really start to make progress in this business.

A recruiter at my firm (who I won't name to spare his blushes) was nowhere for the first six months. He got no traction at all. But he was a hard worker, and he was really committed to improving. So we didn't give up on him. We changed his industry focus, encouraged him to celebrate the small wins along the way, but it was only in year three that it all started to click into place. He's still got a long way to go, but he's putting up solid numbers. His determination and mental toughness are paying off.

This line of work can be a real pressure cooker. You can invest weeks, even months, in a stellar candidate, guide them through ten rounds of interviews, feel like you are right at the finish line . . . only for the company to be acquired, and the whole opportunity vanishes. It can leave you wondering what the point of it all is. That's when you have to dig deep and reconnect with your Why. Why did you choose this profession in the first place? Was it the satisfaction of making a match? The drive to build something? Whatever that core reason is, you have to keep that flame lit.

But perhaps most importantly there has to be an element of commitment. Are you really "all in" on this career? Or are you thinking: *Well . . . I'll keep at it for a year or so, and if it doesn't work out, I'm going to try something else.*

I'll tell you this now: If that's the way you're thinking, you might as well as move on now, because if you've got one foot in and one foot out, you're not going to go the distance.

Do you know the story of the Spanish conquistador, Hernán Cortés? When he landed in Mexico, he ordered his ships to be burned, so they had no way of returning home. They were either going to conquer or die. When you think you've got an "out," you'll subconsciously hold something in reserve, and that can be the difference between success and failure. You have to be all in. You have to have that do-or-die attitude.

Appreciating the small wins along the way helps. Did you connect with a difficult-to-reach candidate? Did you gain some valuable market intelligence? Did you overcome an objection from a hiring manager? Celebrate those moments. They provide the fuel to keep going through the tougher times.

Ultimately, the mental aspect of recruiting comes down to perseverance, resilience, and an unshakeable belief in what you're doing. Recognize that every rejection brings you closer to a placement, and the ability to pick yourself up and keep pushing forward is what distinguishes those who merely survive in this business from those who truly thrive.

It's a marathon, not a sprint, and only a strong mind will carry you across the finish line.

# Chapter 16

# Developing Habits That Become a Routine

How's your daily structure going? Remember back in Chapter Twelve, we talked about the importance of setting up your day with purpose, blocking out specific chunks of time for crucial activities like marketing and recruiting calls, and then allocating other slots for the necessary admin, research, and follow-up?

How are you getting on with actually implementing this structure and taming the daily chaos of your business?

I hope you've at least tried to put this into practice, but don't feel bad if you've already slipped back into bad habits and started bouncing again. It happens to the best of us.

This bouncing thing is so sneaky. You sit down, intending to make your marketing calls, but then an email pings. *Just a quick look*, you tell yourself. Next thing you know, fifteen minutes have vanished, and you're down a rabbit hole, reading about some industry news that could have waited. Then a LinkedIn notification grabs your attention, and *Boom!*—another chunk of your prime phone time is gone. It's incredibly easy to let distractions derail your best intentions.

When I talk to recruiters about this—whether it's to a room of three people or three hundred—when I start describing this bouncing problem, I see heads nodding all over the place. They recognize it because it's a common struggle, especially for those newer to the recruitment game.

Think of your office time as your workout. You don't go to the gym and swim for ten minutes, then hop on the treadmill for five, then do a few bicep curls, and then wander over to the yoga mats. You have to compartmentalize your tasks for efficiency. You dedicate a block of time for cardio, another for strength training, and so on. Your recruiting day is no different. You need those dedicated blocks for specific activities.

Developing these good habits into a solid routine is what separates the recruiters who are just spinning their wheels from those who are actually making placements and building a successful career. It demands mental toughness to stay on your plan and resist those constant distractions.

So, take a moment. Be honest with yourself. Are you controlling your day, or is your day controlling you? Revisit that daily structure we talked about and make a conscious effort to break free from the bounce.

# Chapter 17

# I Found Someone to Market

You feel it in your gut when you connect with a great candidate. Something about the sheen on their resume and the way they talk over the phone. . . . You just know this is a person employers will line up to hire.

That's when you pause and take a second, more objective look. Have you truly found a top-tier candidate, an A player, or is it someone who's just okay, a B player?

Just because someone is qualified on paper and talks a good game doesn't automatically make them an MPC (Most Placeable Candidate).

The real difference will show itself in several key areas:

1. *Motivated:*
   Is this person genuinely driven to make a change, or are they just passively looking? What have they already done to help themselves in their job search? An A candidate is typically proactive and clear about their reasons for wanting a new role.

2.  *Cooperative:*
    Are they easy to work with? Are they responsive? Will they partner with you in the process? An A candidate understands the value of a strong recruiter relationship and is willing to do their part, responding to calls promptly and providing information you need.

3.  *Track Record of Accomplishment:*
    This is crucial. You need to dig deeper than job descriptions alone. What specific impact have they made in their previous roles? Can they quantify their achievements? You want them to brag—you just have to know how to pry it out of them. Ask probing questions like:

    *How do you compare with your peers?*

    *If your boss had to choose between you and someone else for a promotion, why would they choose you?*

4.  *Salary Demands:*
    This one is the make or break, because the compensation a candidate asks for tells you a whole lot more than just their desired income. It's a window into their understanding of their own value and their overall motivations.

    Candidates will often say it's not about the money, but let's be straight, it almost always is. An A candidate, though, usually has a more nuanced perspective than just chasing the biggest paycheck. Look out for these indicators:

    - *Realism:* If a candidate is making $60,000 and wants to make $150,000, that's an obvious red flag. Their expectations are not in line with the market and the kind of role being discussed. We might need to have a candid conversation with them about what is realistic.

- *Motivation:* If the first thing a candidate talks about is wanting more compensation, it could indicate they are primarily driven by money. While understandable, this can make them a higher risk for accepting a counteroffer from their current employer. Their loyalty might just lie with the highest bidder. We want to find candidates who are also motivated by career growth, better culture, or other factors.

- *Truthfulness and Consistency:* This is a big one. We might ask early on what it would take for them to consider a move, and they give us a number, say $110,000. But then, down the line, closer to an offer, they suddenly say they need $120,000 or $125,000 because they *forgot* about a recent raise or they've had a talk with their spouse. That changing of the numbers is a major red flag. It suggests they were not entirely forthright with you from the start, and that erodes trust. Even in today's cut-throat world, you always want to look for candidates that have a sense of honor.

Ultimately, discussing compensation is not just about the dollars and cents. It's about understanding the candidate's drivers, their grasp of reality, and their level of honesty. By asking the right questions, we can get a much clearer picture of whether we have a serious and placeable candidate. It helps us protect our time and avoid those situations where we invest a lot of effort only to have the deal fall apart at the offer stage due to unrealistic or shifting compensation demands.

## Reputation Trumps Fees, Every Time

If you're convinced that you've got an A candidate and you're going to put all your efforts into finding them a role, this is the time to start building your relationship with the client. When you have a true MPC, it's not about getting them into a new position as quickly as possible, hustling for a fee; you want to take the long-term perspective.

In purely practical terms, an MPC may move several more times in their career, especially if they're fairly young, and you want to be the recruiter that they keep coming back to. When you have a great candidate who is smart, dedicated and honorable, you want them to be a success in every possible way. And that means putting them first. Yep, here we go again. . . . It's not about you.

Let me tell you about a guy named Terry.

When I first met him, I could tell straight away that Terry was a really solid professional and a good guy—the kind of individual that had a good head on his shoulders and a strong work ethic—definitely someone who should be considered an A candidate. I was working on a position that seemed like a great fit for his background, and things were progressing well. However, around the same time, Terry was exploring other avenues, and he ended up finding an opportunity on his own.

It was a bit of a heartbreaker because the role I was working on was good, and it was with a client I was really keen to get into a relationship with. Placing Terry with them would have opened a lot of doors.

I'd developed a good rapport with Terry, and I could have easily pushed him to go after my role instead. But it became clear to me that the job Terry had found himself aligned better with his long-term aspirations and his personal circumstances.

Now, as a recruiter, the immediate thought might be: *Well, there goes my fee*. But I realized something crucial: If I pushed Terry hard toward the opportunity I had, even if it meant a quicker placement for me, it wouldn't have been the best thing for him in the long run. True A candidates aren't just looking for any job; they're looking for the right job that fits their specific goals and values. In Terry's case, the opportunity he sourced himself was that better fit.

This was not only the right move from an ethical perspective, putting the candidate first. It was also the smart move in the long-term. Because while I didn't make an immediate placement fee, I built trust with Terry. He now knew, beyond a shadow of a doubt, that I had his best interests at heart.

That's what you should be aiming for in the business. You want to be seen as more than just a transaction. You want people to see you as a friend who just happens to be a recruiter. This is how you escape the stereotype of the devouring recruiter who would sell his grandmother for an easy placement.

I kept in touch with Terry, and a few years later, he went through a tough time with a difficult divorce. I spent hours on the phone with him, even though he wasn't looking for a new role. He needed someone to talk to and, because we had a friendly relationship, I became a listening ear for him.

I remember saying to him, "Tell you what, man, you're going to get married again, and this time it'll be the right one. And when you find the woman that you want to marry, I'll be at the wedding."

I said it to encourage him, but Terry took me seriously. Some years later he did in fact get married again, and sure enough, I got an invite to his wedding. Again, there was no role to fill, and no new fee I was working on. But I said I'd be there, and I was true to my word. I flew out to Kentucky, and I had the privilege of seeing him make his vows.

Think about that for a moment . . .

How many recruiters do you know who have such a good relationship with their candidates that they get an invite to their wedding? It's unheard of, right? But it happened to me. And if you're willing to put in the effort and put your candidates' welfare ahead of your need to earn some commission, it can happen to you too.

And, oh yes. . . . I met quite a few people at Terry's wedding who were in a similar line of work as him. They were intrigued to meet a recruiter who was welcomed at their buddy's wedding. That's a reputational boost you cannot buy. In my book, the good relationship I've enjoyed with Terry and the reputation I've earned as an honest, decent recruiter who puts his candidates first is worth way more than the fee I lost on that first role.

So, when you're assessing a candidate, dig deep with your questions, and don't settle for surface-level answers. Understand their Why. And when you find those A players—the ones who aren't just placeable, but who you can genuinely get excited about marketing because you know they're the real deal—remember that you can never go wrong by doing them right. The best thing you can do for your candidate, and ultimately for your own reputation, is to ensure they find the right fit for them, even if it's not the role that benefits you.

# Chapter 18

# The Art of Asking Questions

If you want to accelerate your progress as a recruiter, getting better at asking questions is one of the best areas to focus on. You can build better networks, uncover hidden placement opportunities, and identify dud deals that you can safely ditch, all by developing this single skill.

It isn't just that asking great questions is effective, it's that so many recruiters struggle with this. It's one of the fastest ways to move out of the *Rookie Zone*, chiefly because so few have the commitment or the drive to get better at this. Because it's not easy. It takes gumption and persistence to ask questions, and then ask more questions, and then ask more questions. Initially it feels uncomfortable. As if you're some kind of interrogator. Can you really just keep asking questions until the other person tells you they're out of time? Yes, you can. And you're going to keep doing it until it becomes natural and conversational.

When you improve in this area, you'll notice your calls get longer, and your relationships become more personable. New recruiters tend to get so focused on their CDS that they finish the prescribed questions and then they freeze. They don't know what else to ask, so they default to asking for an email address and hoping that the other person might later volunteer something useful of their own accord. Spoiler alert: They won't.

In Chapter Thirteen I gave you an extensive list of questions to try, and it's good to have these prompts on hand so you know what to ask next. But eventually you want to be able to ask questions naturally based on the flow of the conversation and motivated by simply being inquisitive. A common pitfall is the *bashful syndrome*, as I call it.

Recruiters, especially when their confidence isn't quite there, hesitate to ask what they think might be a tough question. But the question you don't ask is always the one that comes back to haunt you. It's the one that bites you in the tail every single time. So, you've got to have the courage to ask. There is, of course, a balance to strike. While we're digging for information, we also need to bring value to the person we're speaking with. It can't just be a one-way interrogation. If all you're doing is asking questions without offering any insight or potential help, folks are going to tune out pretty quick. You've got to be thinking about how you can help that person and share useful information with them.

When you're having a conversation, there are three main categories of questions you should be thinking about:

1. *Questions About the Person You're Speaking To:*
   For candidates, this includes their history, their accomplishments, their motivations for wanting to make a move, and what they like and dislike about their current situation. You need to fill out that Candidate Data Sheet thoroughly. For employers, questions about the role they're trying to fill, the type of candidate they're looking for, what they've done so far to fill the role, and the negative effects they're experiencing from not filling the role.

2. *Bracketing Questions:*
   Identify other people this person knows who might be of interest to you. Who do they know that you don't know?

3.  *Movement in the Marketplace:*
    This last category is another one of those key skills that I'll keep returning to. It means figuring out where people are interviewing, which companies are hiring, who's leaving their roles, and where they're going. When you talk to someone, even if they aren't a fit for your current search, you need to ask:

    *Has your company hired anyone recently?*

    *Where did they come from?*

    *Has anyone left your company?*

    *Where did they go?*

    These questions help you follow the breadcrumbs to find out which other companies might be hiring and which candidates may have recently become available.

It's perfectly fine to have a list of possible questions at hand. But in the long run, you want to develop a mindset of constant curiosity and a genuine desire to understand the market and the people in it. Listen intently to the answers and know what to ask next to dig deeper. Bring value while also gathering information.

You'll know when you're improving in this area—first, because you'll consult your list of questions less, and second, you'll ask more questions off the cuff because you recognize that they're the queries that are going to turn up gold. When you master this art, you'll go from being a rookie who runs out of things to say to a seasoned recruiter who uncovers the opportunities and talent that others miss.

# Chapter 19

# The Art of Asking Questions – Gathering Marketing Intel

If it feels like being a successful recruiter means becoming a mixture of entrepreneur, salesperson, marketer, coach, and therapist, you'll be pleased to hear that you can also add professional investigator to the list of skills you need to develop.

Did I mention that making it as a recruiter is hard?

You're only going to get to speak to a handful of people on the phone each day, and most of the time, their responses will be negative. The employer doesn't have any roles to fill, and the candidate isn't interested in changing jobs. A green recruiter hears no and thinks the call is dead. They surrender and say: *Okay, well, if you think of anyone, give me a call.*

I promise this is true: No recruiter who has ever said this to someone has actually gotten a call back. Okay, I guess it's possible that it may have happened to a recruiter once, somewhere in the world, but the chances are good it hasn't happened to you or anyone you know.

So, ditch that line, and instead take a no as an invitation to do some digging. Because every single phone call is an opportunity to extrapolate information that can lead you from a recruiting dead end to a marketing intel goldmine. I've already used the phrase *movement in the marketplace* a few times, but let's really dig into what this means and why it's something you should always be looking for.

*Movement in the marketplace* is what happens when an employee is hired or leaves a role. As soon as that happens, a chain reaction begins that can result in a dozen different people changing roles.

Let's say, for example, that a senior manager at Company A retires, opening up a key vacancy. The company decides to promote from within, and a middle manager moves into that slot. They've now left behind a management role that needs filling, and for this, Company A headhunts a seasoned pro from Company B. Company B now has a vacancy that needs filling, so they advertise the position online and ultimately end up interviewing six candidates. One of the candidates gets the job (leaving an open vacancy at Company C); two of them shrug their shoulders and carry on in their current role while the other three are disappointed and are now motivated to find another similar, new role.

Now imagine that you had spoken to the original senior manager just at the point where he was thinking of retiring. If you're not paying attention, you could assume that this person isn't hiring and isn't looking for a new role. But if you're on the ball, your antennae prick up and you think: *Ah, movement in the marketplace is about to happen.*

You keep talking to the imminent retiree and discover that they're planning to fill the role internally but that this is going to leave a middle-management vacancy. You get the name of the hiring manager, and you now have a juicy lead to follow.

Or perhaps you come in a bit later, and the roles are already filled. Did you come in too late? No! Movement in the market is happening. You find out which company the new hire came from, and now you have a lead for a firm, Company B, which has a role that needs filling.

You call Company B and they've already hired someone. Time to give it up? No! How many candidates did they interview? Six, eh? Who were the candidates that would have been second- and third-place options if the prime candidate fell through? Time to give them a call and offer to help them take the next step in their career.

See how this works? Ask the right questions, do some digging, and you could be the first recruiter to find out who is hiring, who is leaving their role, and who is interviewing. This intel is how you uncover hidden opportunities and pick up fresh leads to follow, often before any other recruiter is even aware of it.

Back when I started in this business, finding any lead meant cracking open the Yellow Pages and making cold call after cold call. You'd flip through those thick books, call a number, and hope somebody on the other end could tell you anything useful. You made a hundred calls, hoping to talk to maybe fifteen people. Today, we have LinkedIn and databases, sure, but the fundamental need to ask the right questions to uncover what's really happening hasn't changed one bit.

So, when an employer says they don't need your candidate, or they don't have an opening right now, you pivot. You say something like:

> *Okay, I understand you don't need my candidate right now, and that's fine. But while I have you on the phone, maybe you could direct me a bit here?*

Then you launch into the questions designed to identify that movement:

*Has your company hired anyone in the last six months?*
If yes: *Who did they hire, and where did they come from?*

*Has anybody left your company in a while?*
If yes: *Where did they go?*

*Have you filled any positions internally?*
If yes: *Has this created a vacancy somewhere?*

*Have you interviewed any candidates recently? What was the outcome? Are there any candidates still in process? Did you interview anyone recently that you couldn't hire, that you really liked? Who were they?*

*Are there any other recruiters working on this position?*

This constant gathering of intel, even from calls that initially seem unproductive, is how you build your "perpetual plan." You're always adding new names of potential candidates or clients to your list. And, instead of just making blind, random calls, you're making contact with places you suspect have activity. This can actually help you avoid that burnout that hits so many recruiters when they feel like they're working hard but spinning their wheels and getting nowhere.

Everybody in your specialist industry knows something about what's happening in their marketplace. Your job is to extrapolate that information. By asking enough questions, you ferret out what's really going on. People don't always tell you the whole story upfront. But if you're friendly and you make a pal, they start to open up and share crumbs of gossip about things happening at their company or even a competitor.

This is the core of gathering marketing intel when you encounter a no. It's transforming every conversation into an opportunity to identify where the action is in the market, building your network, and uncovering those hidden leads that other recruiters miss because they stop asking questions after the first no.

# Chapter 20

# Getting the Most Out of Every Conversation

If you've worked in sales prior to becoming a recruiter, you have a certain advantage because you've probably already learned a lot about the value of asking questions. It's like the job interview question in which the employer asks the candidate to "sell me this pen." In case you're not aware, the correct response is to put the pen to one side and ask something like: *So tell me what you're looking for in a pen today?*

That's Sales 101. Find out what the customer needs and then explain why your product fills that need better than anything else.

I've seen the other side of this when going to a car dealership. I can't resist admiring the flashy sports car, and what does the salesman do? He immediately starts telling me about the horsepower, the acceleration, the leather seats, the whole nine yards. He's in sales mode right away.

But what did he fail to do?

He failed to ask me anything about my situation. He should be asking:

*What kind of car are you looking for today?*

*Where are you going to drive it?*

*How many people are in your family?*

*Are you married—what does your significant other want you to buy?*

He just assumed that, because I looked at a sports car, that's what I wanted. And because he assumed, he wasn't talking to my actual need. He wasn't finding out what I really wanted.

This is precisely the trap recruiters can fall into, and as a result, they fail to get the most out of every conversation.

When you're talking to an employer about a candidate you're marketing, and they say, "Tell me more," all they've done is glance at the sports car. It sounds promising, right? You get excited. So, you pull the hammer back on the machine gun and fire off every great bullet point about their candidate.

You tell them everything the candidate has done, all their accomplishments, their whole background. But you don't know what the employer has already done to try and fill their role, or even if they have one. You don't know because you haven't asked. You're shooting blind.

Instead, when they say, "Tell me more," you have to flip it. It's an opportunity to ask them questions to understand their situation and their needs. You say:

*I'd love to tell you more about the candidate, but before I do, maybe you could share some information with me about what you're looking for so we can determine if this is going to be a good fit for both of us? Are you actually looking for someone right now?*

If they indicate that they have a vacancy or that they're thinking of expanding their team, keep asking questions:

*What kind of experience are you looking for in a candidate?*

*What have you done so far to fill the role?*

*Are you working with any other recruiters?*

What you're doing is determining if they're a tire kicker or if they have a real opening. Your time is valuable, and the worst thing you can do is waste your efforts on someone who is just trying to tap you for details.

The same principle applies when you're recruiting a candidate. You have a great opportunity, you give them the grabber—that impressive selling point—and they say, "Yes, I'm interested," or "Whaddya got?"

That isn't the time to start unloading all the details about the job. You have to find out *why* they're interested in learning more. Get them talking about their situation and their reasons for being interested. You already know something about them, or you wouldn't have called, but you need to know a lot more:

*What's your current employment situation?*

*What is it that's motivating you to look for a new role?*

*What have you done so far to try to find a new role?*

This isn't just about uncovering market movement (although, as we discussed in the previous chapter, that's always something to look out for). This is about understanding the individual—their needs, their wants, their potential obstacles, their hopes, dreams, and desires. You're trying to get a feel for the candidate or the employer, so you can figure out if there's a potential match here, or if they might be in the market for something else you can find for them.

You're squeezing every possible nuance and value out of the conversation. But more than that, you're also demonstrating your worth and separating yourself from other recruiters. When you ask questions with quality and depth, you stop sounding like a recruiter and become more like a consultant or an expert. That's a great place to get to if you want your candidates and employers to respect you and value your opinion.

Many recruiters become so obsessed with making a fee and hitting their targets that they rush their conversations and push people into a quick yes or no. They forget that recruitment is not about them. It's about improving the lives of the candidates and the employers. And you can't do that if you don't take the time in every conversation to add value and build a relationship.

Get this right, and I promise that eventually those placements will come. And better still, it'll happen organically, in a way that will open more doors and make your job easier, not to mention more enjoyable. One placement will lead to a recommendation, which leads to another candidate, which leads to another placement, which leads to a new client.

Try this the next time you take a call. Make a conscious effort to forget about the sale and your targets. And instead, get genuinely curious about the person you're speaking to and how you might be able to help them. If you can do this, you should immediately notice an uptick in the quality and usefulness of your conversations.

# Chapter 21

# Closing Questions to Protect Your Time

At any given time you might have a dozen clients you're trying to recruit for and two to three times as many candidates you're trying to place. These are all opportunities to make a deal and earn a commission.

And most of them will *never* pan out.

We all know this to be true, but we rarely acknowledge this, and we certainly don't act as if this were true. We convince ourselves that we have a chance of converting every opportunity into a sale, and we even crunch the numbers on the back of an envelope to figure out how much commission we're going to get if we win every single one of them.

When I tell recruiters this, their counter is that we have to work this way. We don't know which opportunities will land and which ones won't, so we have to tackle them all with energy and belief to ensure that at least some of them will close.

This is total nonsense.

Yes, certainty doesn't exist in this game, but we can get pretty darn close to it. If we're honest, once we've been recruiting for even just a year or two, we can look at every opportunity we're working on and know, with a pretty high degree of accuracy, which ones have a really strong chance of working out and which ones are a longshot.

"Yes, but—but—there's always a chance, right?"

Yes. There's also a chance of surviving jumping out of a plane without a parachute, but I wouldn't recommend it.

When you first start out, you need to work on every lead that comes your way. It's how you learn. But eventually you can get a feel for which opportunities are, well, actual opportunities, and which ones are pipedreams.

And what happens if you stop working on the pipedreams?

You have more time for working on the real opportunities.

Look at it like this: Would you rather have twenty leads, each of which has a 10 percent chance of working out, or three leads, each of which has a 90 percent chance of working out?

Rookies will take the twenty leads because they believe they can buck the trend, roll the dice, and convert more of those twenty leads than the two that are the statistical likelihood. Honestly, you'd get better odds in Vegas.

The seasoned recruiter, however, knows that the three leads are going to result in two to three placements, making them at least as good as the twenty leads. But it's going to take them considerably less time and effort.

This matters—especially if you want to improve your conversions and your sales targets. Because when you learn to take on the good leads and reject the poor ones, you spend less time spinning your wheels and more time enjoying wins.

It's actually another reason recruiters burn out. They gather scores of leads, and they work on tons of opportunities, so they feel like they're winning. If they can just increase their closing rate, they'll soon be swimming in commissions. But that closing rate never increases, at least not enough to make a real difference. Not because they're bad at sales, but because they're burning time and energy on opportunities that even the greatest recruiter of all time couldn't close. Eventually, the frustration mounts and the recruiter tires of working longer and longer days and never seeing any advancement.

When I train recruiters, there are a handful of mantras that I continually repeat, to the point where people tire of hearing them. But that's good. Because when a recruiter wearies of me repeating myself, that's when I know they've internalized it.

You've already heard me keep repeating things like, *Master the art of asking questions* or *Identify movement in the marketplace*. But one of the other big ones I'm going to keep coming back to is:

*Protect your time.*

Because the vast majority of what we do is on a contingency basis, we don't get paid a dime unless we make a placement. This means we invest our most valuable, and frankly, our only truly finite asset—our time—upfront, for free, without any guarantee of a return.

Candidates and employers alike, however, won't think twice about wasting your time. They'll burn through your minutes without a second thought if you let them. People will call you, wanting information, wanting to know what's happening in the market, maybe just kicking tires or looking for gossip, but they have no real intention or motivation to make a change or fill a position. They simply want to extract what knowledge they can from you. That's not a criticism. Most people outside the industry don't know how recruitment works, so they don't appreciate the problems it causes a recruiter when they string them along with maybes and might-dos.

The key for us is to figure out as early as possible who is genuinely serious, who is truly motivated, and where there is real urgency before you commit significant time and effort. And the answer lies in the quality of the questions you ask (there's that mantra again!). Get this right, and the candidate will soon reveal whether they're an MPC or someone you shouldn't be wasting time on. Or whether they're a great company to recruit for, rather than a nightmare that rejects every candidate you ever send them because they weren't serious about making a new hire.

I've labelled these as *Closing Questions* because they tend to come at the end, after you've already generated enough rapport with the individual to be able to probe a bit. But don't mistake these as routine questions included simply to complete a form. These are highly strategic questions designed to help you make an educated decision about whether to invest your valuable time in that particular candidate or employer. You decide if you want to engage. They don't get to call the shots on whether they work with you.

*What have you done to help yourself thus far?*

You've seen this question already, but I want you to reframe it in your mind as an opportunity to rate the quality of this lead. It's perhaps the most important question you can ask, and it works for both candidates and for employers, so you can use it on every call with a new prospect.

For candidates their answer reveals a great deal about their motivation and seriousness. If they tell you they're miserable in their current role, desperate to leave, but they haven't even updated their resume, haven't spoken to any other recruiters, haven't had an interview, haven't asked their friends about opportunities. . . . What does that tell you?

It suggests they may not be truly motivated to make a change right now. They might be unhappy, but they haven't taken the steps to actually do anything about it. Investing significant time in someone who isn't driving their own process is a risk for your time.

Now, flip that question to the employer side. Again, the answer provides crucial insight into their level of urgency and potential roadblocks. If they say they are just getting started—or worse, that the position has been open for six months—recognize the warning signals. If a position has been open a long time, despite them claiming "incredible urgency," you have to ask why. Often it's because the compensation is too low for the market. This is a red flag—something that, unfortunately, you're not going to be able to fix.

I've seen recruiters waste their time on these leads because they assume that having a position open for a long time means they must be desperate. Nope. If they've been able to manage this long without that role filled, how important can it really be? Certainly not important enough to pay market rates or better, because otherwise they would have filled it already. See how this works? There's no point in beating your head against a wall on a position with an employer's unrealistic compensation expectations.

We're back to this notion of good recruiters being good investigators. Your goal is to uncover the truth. You keep asking questions, digging deeper, until you have the full picture. This isn't being nosy for the sake of it. You're gathering the necessary intelligence to help you make sound decisions about where to focus your attention.

Here are a bunch more questions. Don't treat this as a list you have to reel off like a robot. Instead, study these questions and get a feel for the information you're trying to dig up. And then think about what the responses will reveal about the level of seriousness and commitment the individual has. When you're an experienced, high-quality recruiter, it's a privilege to work with you. It's not something you offer to everyone who says they might need your help someday. You want people who are eager, motivated, and ready to take action now.

## Candidate Closing Questions

- *Have you prepared a resume?*

- *Are you working with any other recruiters? If so, where have you been submitted? What's your status with those recruiters?*

- *Have you forwarded your resume anywhere else, e.g., to potential employers, other recruiters, friends, or contacts?*

- *Have you interviewed anywhere in the past six months?*

- *Have you received any offers? With whom? What's the status of those offers?*

- *Have you turned down any offers, and if so, why?*

- *What have you done to try to correct the problem with your current employer?*

- *What level of compensation do you need me to negotiate on your behalf?*

- *If I agree to help you find your dream role, will you agree to return calls and emails within twenty-four hours?* (You're exchanging commitments.)

- *Can I have your cell number?*

## Employer Closing Questions

- *How long has the position been open?*

- *What is the critical date by which the position needs to be filled?*

- *What happens if you don't fill the position?*

- *How much money is it costing you/your company for this position to remain unfilled?*

- *Are there any other recruiters working on this position? If so, what's the candidate flow like from them?*

- *Have you interviewed any candidates? What were the outcomes? Are any candidates still in process?*

- *Have you made any offers? What happened? Did someone turn it down? Was it lost to a counteroffer? Did they want too much money?*

- *If I present a  feedback in twenty-four hours or less. Can you commit to that?* (If they can't commit, or they agree and don't follow through, the urgency isn't real.)

- *Can I have the hiring official's cell number?*

- *Can I have some pre-assigned interview times, say two one-hour slots on a specific day?*

To begin with, when you sense weakness in urgency and motivations, it can be hard to turn down the opportunity. Your brain will keep telling you that *there's always a chance*. But it gets easier over time. Eventually, you'll ask some of the above questions, hear the answers, and know with a high degree of certainty that this is going to suck up your time for weeks or even months, and you're going to have nothing to show at the end of it.

If it helps, work out roughly how many hours you're going to need to put into this opportunity, and then use your average hourly rate to convert that into a dollar amount. Then ask yourself: *Am I willing to gamble this amount of money on making a placement here?*

Time is money, right? So, we shouldn't be gambling with it unless we have a high degree of certainty that it's going to pay out.

Of course, sometimes, despite asking the right questions, circumstances can change, or you might get fooled. That's fine. There's no such thing as absolute certainty on either side of the equation. The goal is to make a conscious, educated choice based on the information you gather, rather than blindly investing your time and hoping for the best.

Every recruiter has the same number of minutes in a day. Being efficient with that time by protecting it is how you achieve success. And you protect it by taking control of the qualification process.

# Chapter 22

# Taking a Complete Job Order – Expanding the Search Parameters

Do you want to double the number of targeted candidates you find for your client, and do so before most other recruiters have finished brushing the breakfast crumbs off their hoodie?

This is so easy to do, and it all comes back to how well you have completed the original job order.

I hope by now you've become pretty competent at taking a really thorough job order (see Chapter Five), you've expanded the range of questions you ask to the point where you know everything it's possible to know about the role you're trying to fill, and who and what the client is looking for. The next level of skill for taking a job order is helping the client adjust their expectations while also expanding their openness about what is and isn't available.

In other words, you're going to take charge of the conversation and *expand the search parameters* so they're agreeable to seeing a greater variety of candidates.

This is in everyone's best interest. It's good for you, because a wider brief makes it easier to find candidate matches. It's good for your candidates, because they get the opportunity to go after more roles. And it's good for the employers, because they greatly increase the chances that they're going to find a great fit, nice and early in the process.

The reason this strategy works is that, much of the time, you'll be presented with a job order that seems, shall we say . . . a bit ambitious. The employer has this golden image in their mind of a candidate who is twice as skilled and experienced as the last person in the role, someone who is willing to work for half the salary.

And I'm only slightly exaggerating.

It's your job as an expert in recruitment to help the employer set realistic expectations. You might be able to find that one-in-a-million for them, but it's usually better for everyone if you find them a strong candidate today, rather than shooting for an unreachably high standard and risk never finding a candidate that can match those dreams.

The most common way this manifests is when the employer lists four or five *critical skills*, and they say they want candidates who have abilities and experience in *all* of them. If you know that candidates in this industry, with this variety and depth of experience, are almost nonexistent, it's your duty to say something.

That doesn't mean you should tell the client that they're crazy and they need to lower their expectations. But you also don't have to just nod along. Instead, ask clarifying questions. For instance:

> *Which of those required skills/experiences is the most important to you and which ones could you live without?*

If they insist that they're all too important to leave out, try asking:

> *Which skills could you train them to do on the job?*

Once you've gotten them to bend on one or two of the required skills, you can ask something like:

> *If I find a candidate who is really strong on three out of the four skills and are willing to undergo training to learn the fourth, would you want to meet them?*

When they agree, you can even push a little further:

> *What if I find a candidate who is really experienced in two of the required skills, is willing to do training to get up to speed on the other two, and is in the sweet spot for salary levels, and so forth? Would you reject them out of hand, or would you still want to meet them?*

This helps you identify the absolute nonnegotiables versus the nice-to-haves, giving you more flexibility in your search.

Pushing back on salary can also be a great way to expand your field of candidate possibilities. This is another area in which employers often have unrealistic expectations.

Maybe their previous employee in the role was with them for ten years and only got small salary bumps. So the employer is unprepared for the current market rate. In fact, the previous employee might have left precisely because the employer was paying too far below market rates, and they got a better offer.

You know the market. You know what top people are making. You have an opportunity here to help the employer appreciate how realistic—or unrealistic—their expectations are.

You can use illustrations, such as asking them about the last time they bought a car—the price of a car from five years ago isn't the price today, and the same applies to talent in the marketplace. You can then use the same technique as above to push the envelope:

> *So, although the salary target is $125,000, if I find that superstar who's already making $140,000? Do you want to talk to that person?*

If they say yes, you've just effectively expanded the real compensation range.

If they are rigid and insist that $125,000 is all they have in the budget, and you know you can't find the person they need for that price, that's a red flag. You might have to be upfront and tell them that this isn't something you can recruit on. You're all about protecting your time, remember? Don't commit to trying to find a candidate when you know the salary cap is totally unrealistic. It's okay to say no. Better to disappoint them now rather than in three months after you've wasted hours and hours of work looking for a candidate who doesn't exist.

Now look for other opportunities to expand the search parameters. Over time you'll get a feel for when the employer has a genuine "red line" about things like length of experience, formal qualifications, salary expectations, working location, and when flexibility is possible. Don't make assumptions, but gently prompt the employer with the same question:

> *I appreciate that X is really important to you for this role, but if I find an amazing candidate who is Y, would you still want to meet them?*

Most employers will hate the idea of missing out on a potentially brilliant candidate just because they're slightly lacking in one area and readily agree.

And just like that, you've expanded your potential pool of candidates and made everyone's life a heck of a lot easier.

# Chapter 23

# Handling the "What's Your Fee?" Question

I'm going to share a sales truism with you that you might already know if you've been in the game a while. So, apologies if you're familiar with this, but it's important for every recruiter to be aware. I'm amazed at how often I tell people about this, and they say they believe me, only to completely forget everything I've said when they come across it in the real world.

It's when someone says:

*What's your fee?*

To the uninitiated, this sounds like someone is about to make a purchase. All you have to do is tell them the fee, and the deal's done!

But that isn't what's happening. What they're really trying to find out is whether what you charge has any connection to the quality and level of the service you appear to be offering. And the *earlier* they ask this question—since they don't know at this stage more than the fact that you're a recruiter—the more likely they're either going to use your answer as an excuse to exit the conversation or as a foothold to explain why you're charging too much and you need to discount it before they'll even consider it.

This makes sense in the abstract, but when you've just made twenty phone calls with no reply, and you've finally managed to find a person to speak to, it's so hard not to respond to this question by immediately blurting out something like:

*Oh, we charge* 25 percent *of the base salary.*

And now you're well and truly caught in the trap. The conversation immediately stops being about the value you can bring and how you can solve their problem and instead becomes a negotiation.

*Well, every other recruiter we work with charges 20 percent.*

Now you're stuck arguing over nickels before you've even shown them you're worth a dime.

So, what's the move? Simple. You absolutely do not, under any circumstances, discuss your fee until you have *all* the details of the role, the employer, the type of candidate they're looking for, what they've done so far to fill the role, and so on. All the questions that, by now, should be rolling off your tongue with ease.

You can simply tell the employer this is the case. The phrase I teach, the one that has proven its worth time and again, is:

*I can't quote you a fee until I have a better understanding about the position you're trying to fill and determine whether or not my candidate is a fit.*

This isn't just kicking the can down the road. This response is your opportunity to pivot and take a full job order. Now you're immediately separating yourself from the pack. While lesser recruiters are just dumping candidate information or haggling over a percentage, you're going to start asking all of the usual questions and dig until you hit bedrock.

When you're taking the job order and asking a myriad of questions to determine what the employer actually needs, you're demonstrating your expertise. Recruiters who ask meaningful, smart questions come across as interested and professional, and this is going to make justifying your fee much easier when you eventually share this with the client. In fact, if you do this with enough skill and confidence, it's amazing how often there's no pushback on price, even if your fee is higher than average. When people really want what you're selling, and they truly believe you can deliver, they're far less inclined to quibble over a few percentage points.

The questions to ask are discussed in earlier chapters, so I won't list them all again now, but one question you may want to add into the mix is:

*How much is it costing you per month to have this position remain unfilled?*

This is a great question to ask because when they quantify that cost—and it can be substantial, perhaps tens of thousands of dollars a month—you can then refer to it when you enter the negotiation phase. Your fee is no longer just transactional, a candidate-for-cash arrangement. It's an investment to stop the bleeding.

*Okay, so it's costing you $20,000 a month, and it's been open for six months. That's $120,000 you've already lost. If I can fill this position in, say, one month, instead of it potentially staying open for several more, my fee of, let's say, $30,000 for a $100,000 salary is far less than the money you're losing if this role remains vacant.*

Another of my favorite points is:

> *You're not paying me just for finding a person. You're paying me for the solution to your problem, which is bringing in someone who will be productive and stopping that financial rot.*

It can be difficult initially to bring yourself to sidestep the question about your fee. But keep reminding yourself that, in sales, telling the prospect that you need more information before you can give them a quote or an estimate is normal.

> *I will go through the fees with you in a moment, but I just have a few questions I need to cover first.*

By gathering all this intelligence before you talk numbers, you're showing the client you're a serious professional. You understand the complexities of executive search. Your fee, when it's eventually presented, usually within a fee agreement that needs to be signed before you submit a candidate's name or resume, is justified by the value you deliver—finding the solution to their specific, well-understood, and costly problem.

Recruiting for this role isn't something they could easily do themselves, or they wouldn't be talking to you.

This process also allows you to decide whether you actually want to invest your time in this client and this search. Your time and expertise are valuable. The client isn't the only one deciding whether you'll work together. There are a million recruitment opportunities for you out there, so they need you far more than you need them. That doesn't mean you should be arrogant or dismissive, but you should never create the impression that they'll be doing you a favor by using your service. The power balance is always in your favor.

The next time that "What's your fee?" question comes, don't flinch. Don't take the bait and fall into the trap. This is your chance to show them you're not just another recruiter, wallpapering inboxes with resumes. You're a professional problem-solver.

Take that complete job order, uncover the urgency and the cost of inaction, and set the stage for a successful partnership.

# Chapter 24

# Raising Your Game

When I first started as a recruiter in 1985, I did pretty well the first year. I placed about a dozen people and billed around $125,000. If you've been in this game for a while, you'll know that this is unusual. Most recruiters take a few years before they break the six-figure barrier. So don't be disheartened if it takes you time to get up to speed. This is normal.

But I'm going to share a couple of closing techniques that will help you get there a heck of a lot faster.

I came up with these strategies around year five. I was hitting around $180,000 a year in billing, which was enough to get me a decent place on the office leaderboard and qualify me for the annual trips. But I felt like I'd plateaued. I knew, instinctively, that I was leaving money on the table, I just needed to figure out how and why.

It helped that it was a competitive office, so I could see the heights that other, more experienced, recruiters were reaching. I could see what was possible, and I wanted to be right up there with them.

And these closes made it happen.

I've summarized them below, but as you're reading, see if you can figure out what they both have in common.

## The Takeaway Close

If I'm talking to a candidate or an employer, and I sense they're hesitating or maybe waffling a little bit about an opportunity, I simply stop pushing. I say something like:

> *You know, this doesn't sound like it's the right opportunity for you. Maybe we should just move on and forget about it.*

One of two things will happen next. If the candidate or employer is genuinely interested, they'll let you know in a hurry. Human nature is funny. When you start to take something away from someone, it suddenly becomes more valuable to them. The fear of missing out kicks in, and if they really want it, they'll say so.

Alternatively, the person might agree with you, in which case you've just identified that this person was never really interested in the first place. They were just stringing you along or kicking the tires. Disappointing, obviously, but at least now you know, and you can move on to finding better opportunities.

## The Sharp Angle Close

The Sharp Angle Close method is all about exchanging commitments. It's the idea expressed by: *If I do this for you, will you do this for me?*

In practice, this means laying out your expectations upfront. If you're talking to a candidate, and they seem interested, but you want to be sure, you say:

*Look, I'm gonna go ahead and put a marketing plan together for you. In the meantime, you need to get me your resume, okay? When can I have that by?*

*No, end of the week is too long, we need to move quickly. Can you get it to me by the end of the day? Good.*

*And just to be clear, if you don't follow through on your end, I'm just gonna assume you're no longer interested in moving forward with this. I'll consider the matter closed.*

And it works the same way with the employers too:

*I'm going to start sending you candidates in the next day or two. I need you to commit to responding within twenty-four hours.*

*Can you do that? Good.*

*And just to be clear, if you don't follow through on your end, I'm just gonna assume you're no longer interested in moving forward with this. I'll consider the matter closed.*

What this does is let me figure out early on if a candidate or an employer is committed to the process, or if they're just wasting my time. We call chasing deals that don't have a real shot, *riding the dead bull*, and every recruiter has to deal with these. The candidate can sound enthusiastic, the employer can sound professional, but after a few weeks of unreturned calls and playing email ping-pong, you have to accept that this opportunity is never going to close.

The Sharp Angle Close doesn't bring a dead bull back to life, but what it achieves, really effectively, is to tip you off that it's deceased early in the process. Really, how hard is it for a candidate to update their resume and email it over? Or for an employer to send an email saying either the candidate isn't a good fit or that they'd like to interview them? Not hard at all. So, if they can't manage those things, the odds that they're ever going to turn into a fee is close to zero.

What you're effectively doing here is forcing the person's hand. They now have no choice but to make it very clear by their action just how committed they really are.

## A More Efficient Hunter

Can you see the common thread between these two closes?

It's the "protecting your time" mantra that we discussed in Chapter Twenty-One. Both of these strategies allow you to get rid of the dead wood and stop wasting time on opportunities that are likely never going to close.

Remember, it does no good to ride a dead bull just because there's a 1 percent chance that they'll close. Because that means you'd need to work 100 of these terrible projects just to make one placement!

Here's a fun exercise. Estimate how many hours you spend on the average project that starts promisingly and then fizzles out a few weeks or months later. Now, multiply that by one hundred. That's how much time it will take you to earn a single commission from a dead bull.

It's like in the movie *Dumb and Dumber,* when Mary tells Lloyd that there's a one-in-a-million chance they could ever go out together. And Lloyd excitedly shouts, "So, you're telling me there's a chance!"

You've got to get real with yourself. If you acknowledge when an opportunity is a bust and stop kidding yourself that *there's a chance*, you'll become more efficient and have more time to spend on the opportunities that have a reasonable chance of coming together.

Implementing these two closes is a big part of what changed things for me. I stopped letting low-quality opportunities chew up my day, and my billings really started to take off. And they continued to increase significantly, year after year. Our time is the most expensive time there is because we don't get paid unless we make a placement. Weed out the situations that aren't going anywhere, spend more time on real opportunities, and you'll significantly raise your game.

# Chapter 25

# Fee Types – Contingency, Retained, and Priority

Recruiters generally work under one of three types of fee arrangements: *Contingency*, *Retained*, or *Priority* (also referred to as *Engaged*). You're likely familiar with all three, and which one you employ will usually be determined by your recruitment firm. But it's worth reviewing each one briefly, because each one has its own nuances that may not have been explained to you.

## Contingency Search

Contingency Search is far and away the most common arrangement for recruiters in most countries. With Contingency Search, we only get paid if the employer actually hires a candidate that we referred to them. If they don't hire someone from us, we don't get paid.

Usually, the fee is a percentage of the employee's starting salary. Some agencies work on a flat fee, but this is more common when filling unskilled roles at volume and isn't really relevant to the type of relationship-based recruitment you're performing.

There is often also a guarantee period, which is usually thirty to sixty days. If the employee leaves, or is fired, the fee is refunded or the role is recruited again for free. Guarantee periods are sometimes offered for longer periods in exchange for a higher fee percentage. For instance, if you offer an employer a thirty-day guarantee but the employer insists on a longer guarantee, you can offer this in thirty-day increments at an additional charge of 1.5 percent per period. So, in this example, if you're collecting a 30 percent fee, and the employer wants an additional sixty days, you'd charge them 33 percent of the hired candidate's income.

Remember, as recruiters we present qualified, interested, and motivated candidates, but the employer chooses who they ultimately hire. The employer wanting a longer guarantee period is asking the recruiter to provide them insurance against the employer making the right hiring decision. Charge for that insurance.

The main thing to understand with Contingency is that we, the recruiters, are taking all the risk. The employer isn't taking any risk with us because we're working for free unless a placement happens. This is why you have to be sharp and protect your time.

Under this kind of arrangement, the other complication you should watch out for is when an employer is working with multiple recruiters on the same position. Many recruiters will happily join the mob, but that's usually because they're going to just send over a bunch of candidates from their database and hope that their guy or gal candidate gets selected.

But that's not recruitment, that's resume-shuffling.

Usually, the recruiters competing to fill a single slot are going to put minimal effort into finding the right candidate for the employer because they know they have only a small percentage chance of making a fee. There's no incentive for them to put in any real time or effort.

Generally speaking, at WorldBridge, we won't work on a role if there are other recruiters already involved. It's bad for us, it's bad for the employer, and it's bad for the candidates.

Think about it: When you've got multiple recruiters talking to candidates about the same company, are they all saying the same things? Are they protecting that company's brand in the marketplace? You could have mixed signals going out. And the candidates may be getting multiple calls from different recruiters or getting called to interview with a company that is totally ill-suited to what they're looking for. It's a bad look.

And more importantly, for us, it significantly diminishes our chances of success. It's just too many cooks in the kitchen. We work under a contingency arrangement, but it has to be exclusive.

Sometimes we agree to an exclusive arrangement for a limited time—say two weeks or a month—to find qualified candidates. That can work. But there must always be some level of exclusivity.

Your recruitment firm's policy may be different, and they may require you to take on roles, even if other recruiters are involved. How you handle this is up to you, but if you have to take on these low-quality opportunities, I recommend putting as little time into the project as possible in favor of those for which you have exclusivity. Even if your firm insists you participate in these bun-fights, there's nothing to stop you from telling employers that you insist on exclusivity. This should mean that at least you can reduce the frequency with which you have to engage in these pointless exercises.

But what do you do if an employer tells you they aren't working with any other recruiters, and then you find out later they are? This is why asking the right questions upfront is so critical.

When you're taking that job order, you need to ask:

- What have you done to help yourself thus far to fill this position?

- How long has the position been open?

- Have you interviewed any candidates? What was the outcome?

- Are there any candidates still in process?

- Have any other recruiters presented candidates?

These questions make it very difficult for the employer to hide the fact that they've got other recruiters on the case.

If they do manage to slip one by you, and you later find out they weren't square with you, perhaps through the candidate or another source, you have to address it. You've essentially invested your time under a false premise.

This is when you can use the Takeaway Close (see Chapter Twenty-Four):

> *Mr. Employer, you told me this was an urgent situation and that you weren't working with other recruiters, but it appears that wasn't the case. Obviously, this is not as urgent or exclusive as we agreed, so I won't be spending any more time recruiting for this position.*

The employer will either 'fess up and call off the other recruiters, or they'll accept the conclusion, and you at least will have avoided having to waste any more time with a dishonest employer.

## Retained Search

This is also an exclusive arrangement, but in this instance, payment is typically split into thirds. One third up front when you take the job order, another third when you present qualified candidates, and the final third upon placement.

We don't do a whole lot of Retained Searches, primarily because a lot of employers don't like them, but also because, in my opinion, Priority Search (which we'll come on to in a moment) is a more flexible approach.

The risk with Retained Search is that, once that client pays you upfront, you are married to that search. You are committed to working on it and spending significant time on it. But what if afterward you discover that you've saddled up on a dead bull? Maybe the employer turns out to be looking for some kind of pink unicorn that is going to be almost impossible to find. But you've taken a retained fee, so now you're committed to chasing something that doesn't exist.

If you are going to work on retainer (again, this might be standard for your recruitment firm and you might have no choice), be sure to take a detailed job order and to ask a ton of questions. Be extra sure that this is an opportunity you believe you can fill in a reasonable time before you take the first part of the fee.

## Priority (Engaged) Search

This is identical to Contingency Search, except that the client pays a nonrefundable deposit at the beginning. Once the placement is made, this deposit is deducted from the final bill. If the placement isn't made, for any reason, you keep the deposit.

Obviously, this isn't for everyone with an open position. Unsurprisingly, some employers are not going to be wild about this idea. But if a client has shared a serious sense of urgency to fill their position, and they've told you it's costing them big money to have that position sitting empty, this is a great time to introduce this type of fee.

You'll know when an opportunity is ripe for this, because the employer will have indicated that they'd practically crawl across broken glass to get it filled. They've tried posting it on job boards, they've worked with other recruiters, and they just can't find the right person.

When you've taken a complete job order, you've asked all those exhaustive questions to understand their situation, and they've laid out just how urgent this is. This is your moment. You simply ask:

> *Okay, so, where should I send the invoice?*

They're likely gonna look at you funny or ask: *What invoice? I thought you were working on Contingency?* And that's when you lay it out, calmly and clearly:

> *Mr. Employer, you just shared with me that this is an urgent situation, that it's costing you substantially to have this position unfilled. You said you wanted this treated as a priority. So, to escalate our effort and treat this with the priority it deserves, we need to do this as a Priority Search.*

Why does this work? It's all about demonstrating commitment and, frankly, weeding out the tire kickers. Nobody forks over money up front unless they're serious and they believe you can actually bring them a solution.

Think of it like hiring a good attorney. When you need a lawyer for something important, you don't expect them to work for free on the promise you might pay them later if you win the case. This might be true if you're suing someone for whiplash, but if you're fighting a child custody battle or you've been wrongfully charged with a serious crime, you're going to pay a retainer. You're paying for their dedicated time, their expertise, and their intense focus on your problem. They take your case seriously because you've demonstrated you're serious by investing up front.

It's the same principle here. A Priority Search ensures their cooperation and shows they're willing to invest in getting this critical position filled quickly. It also commits them to giving you everything you need to do this search well because they've now got skin in the game. Suddenly you find email requests being responded to quickly and calls returned within the hour.

One of the other major benefits is that it effectively locks out the competition. If I call an employer and they tell me they've already paid another recruiter an engagement fee, I'm staying away. I'm not working on that. It's already covered. A recruiter is going to have a hard time convincing your client that they should ditch you when they've already paid you a substantial, nonrefundable sum.

You also get some level of protection if the situation changes on their end. With contingency, you could bust your tail for weeks, find the perfect candidate, and then the employer hires someone internal, or the boss's family member gets the job. All that time you invested? Gone, zero pay. With a Priority Search, that upfront payment is still in the bank, even if they fill the position themselves or through another source. It ensures that the time, sweat, and effort you've already invested in finding that solution have been paid for.

As you can probably tell, I'm a big fan of Priority Search. But use it wisely; it's not suitable for every project, and if you use it at the wrong time it can turn people away. Once you've told an employer that it has to be a Priority Search, you can't really change tack and say: *I'll do it on contingency, then.* This is actually a type of Sharp Angle Close, so keep this weapon in your armory for when you're working with an employer who says their situation is urgent and you want to be sure they're being straight with you.

In practice, unless you work for yourself, your choice of search and fee type is going to be mostly dictated to you by your recruitment firm. When you've amassed some years of experience and proven yourself to be a top performer, your firm is likely going to give you more leeway with how you negotiate with employers. But if you're still in the rookie phase, you can at least be aware of the pros and cons of each type of search so you can avoid the pitfalls and keep the odds in your favor.

# Chapter 26

# Prepping a Candidate for Initial Interview

Sending a candidate to an interview makes recruiters itchy.

It's one of the key deciders of whether the placement is going to happen, and it's out of our control. We can't be there to prompt the candidate or bail them out if they get bogged down with a tricky question. All we can do is sit and wait for the calls from the candidate and the employer to find out how it went.

It will definitely help your peace of mind if you can accept that you don't have infinite control over the recruitment process, and you can learn to let go of the need to micromanage everything. This often comes with time. So, until then, you can ease a lot of your anxieties by prepping the candidate before the interview happens.

The rookie mistake here is to spend hours with the candidate. This is way too long. In fact, thirty to forty-five minutes is too long. You can't compensate for the fact that you won't be present for the interview by trying to figure out the perfect answer to every potential question the employer might ask. You've got better things to be doing. And besides, the candidate isn't going to remember the majority of what you tell them, so keep it short and sweet, and make sure they're clear on the following three points.

## 1. Accomplishments

The vast majority of the time, the interview isn't going to be conducted by a professional interviewer. Oftentimes, it's an HR person who is mainly interested in trying to screen people out to get the shortlist down to something manageable. And even if it's an interviewer who has expertise in the particular industry and is perhaps going to be the new hire's manager, they're still unlikely to be trained to identify the right candidate. They might do crazy things like hire folks based on whether they went to the same college.

As a result, the best thing you can teach your candidate is how to take control of the interview. You don't want them sitting passively and hoping they get asked the right questions. Instruct the candidate to wait until they're asked the one question that is almost always asked early on:

*Tell me about yourself.*

Most candidates will respond with a summary of their career, a little bit about their hobbies, where they're from, where they went to school, and so on. This is a *huge* waste of everyone's time and misses a golden opportunity to take charge of the interview.

What we need to impress upon the candidate is that the employer has *already* read their resume. They know where the candidate went to school, the jobs they've done previously, their key achievements. Recapping all of that is pointless. What the interviewer *really* wants to know, whether they're aware of it or not, is:

- How well did they care for the duties in their previous roles?

- What kind of person are they?

- What truly motivates them?

- How do they tackle challenges and adversity?

So, when that inevitable first question, "Tell me about yourself," comes up, instead of launching into some long, boring history lesson, they should take control of the conversation in two easy steps:

1.   Give a short accomplishment-focused answer.
2.   Then say this:

> *Mr. Interviewer, I know you've had a chance to review my resume and see my accomplishments. Perhaps it would be easier for you to tell me: What would you like me to accomplish in this position?*

This question is pure, 24 karat gold. Because the employer will then tell the candidate *exactly* what they're looking for. They'll list the key responsibilities, but then also *how* they want the candidate to tackle them. They may reveal details such as the goals for the role, what they hope the long-term success of the role will produce, and how this might tie in to the company's long-term plans.

These are details that might not have come out before, and are going to give the candidate the opportunity to do what most other candidates won't:

> *Sell themselves to the employer based on precisely what the employer is looking for!*

They can give specific examples of how they've achieved similar things in the past, quantifying their success whenever possible, and expressing their enthusiasm for achieving exactly what the employer is looking for.

Can you see how powerful this is? Most candidates, unless they're already a very skilled salesperson, will never think to do this. Which means your candidates are going to have the edge.

Explain this strategy to the candidate but keep it as simple as possible, so it's easy for them to remember:

- Wait until you're asked the "Tell me about yourself" question.

- Give a short, accomplishment-based answer.

- Ask the interviewer what they would like the candidate to accomplish in this role.

- Tell the interviewer why you're the perfect candidate to accomplish these things and give examples from previous roles or projects.

If the candidate remembers nothing else about your interview prep session, and follows through on this one strategy, you've just massively increased their chances of landing the role.

## 2. Problems

The next question for the candidate to ask the interviewer, ideally immediately after they've just performed the above jujitsu, is to ask a new question:

*What are the problems that you're experiencing in filling this position?*

or:

*What challenges will I be expected to tackle in this position?*

The first version is a good one to teach the candidate if you know there have been problems finding the right candidate. Otherwise, instruct them to ask the second question. Either way, the employer will likely tell them what's causing them headaches and what issues the new hire needs to solve.

Again, this gives the candidate the chance to respond by detailing how they've solved similar problems before. This approach shows the candidate is thinking about the employer's needs, not just their own.

Every employer wants someone who can walk in, solve their problems, and make their life easier. By asking this question, the candidate now knows what to tell the employer to convince them that hiring them is going to allow them to sleep better at night.

## 3. Qualifications

The topic of Qualifications is one to save until the end, when the interviewer asks what always signals the interview is coming to an end:

*Do you have any final questions?*

Tell the candidate to respond by asking:

*Do you have any questions about my qualifications or ability to do the job?*

If they don't ask this question, and the employer does have a question or a concern, neither you nor the candidate will hear about it until you get the call advising you that the candidate isn't getting the job. But by asking this, the employer will be prompted to reveal any concerns or clarify anything that might have been missed. It's the candidate's chance to overcome any potential objections right there and then. If the employer says they don't have any questions, the candidate should then ask:

*What are the next steps?*

This shows clear interest, and the interviewer will often tip their hand at this point and hint at how strong the candidate's application is.

## Just Three Words

You can teach the candidate all three of these strategies in less than ten minutes. Tell them to write them down and practice them, either right there and then with you, or with a friend or family member.

The three key words for them to remember are:

- Accomplishments

- Problems

- Qualifications

If they can remember these in the interview, this will remind them of the three questions they need to ask to take control of the process and maximize their ability to convince the interviewer that they're talking to the right person for the job.

## How About No?

Aside from these three key words, there are also a handful of mistakes that you should instruct the candidate to avoid at all costs.

- *Personal and/or Irrelevant*

    Unless the conversation naturally goes there and it's relevant for some reason, the candidate shouldn't dive into their divorce, their church, or other personal details. This is a professional setting. Now, if they discover they both love college football and want to chat about that for a minute, fine. Rapport is good. But stick to professional relevance.

- *Negative or Derogatory Comments*

  The candidate should never, ever badmouth a former boss, company, or colleague. If asked why they're leaving their current role, they should keep it professional and vague:

  > *A recruiter contacted me about an opportunity that looks to be better than the one I'm currently engaged in. I'm here to explore if this is the case.*

- *Discussing Compensation*

  This is absolutely forbidden territory for the candidate in the first interview. Along with the opening "Accomplishments" strategy, this is the element of the interview preparation you must emphasize multiple times.

  The candidate simply doesn't have enough information yet to put a number on their value for this specific opportunity. They could price themselves out by asking too much, or worse, leave money on the table by asking too little.

  Discussing compensation is our job as the recruiter, and the candidate must agree not to get into this with the interview. If the employer presses, the candidate's response should be something like:

  > *I'm not prepared to discuss compensation at this point, I'm here to learn about the opportunity and see if there's a fit.*

  If they keep pushing, and insist on a number, this response usually works:

> *My current compensation is $XXX, but once I've fully understood this opportunity, I'll consider any reasonable offer.*

But under no circumstances should they go any further with this discussion. It usually helps to inform the candidate that, if they do get into the compensation discussion, they will almost certainly end up with an offer that is less than if they let you handle it. This tends to placate the overconfident candidate who might be inclined to ignore your advice.

So, that's all you need to cover. Three key words, don't discuss compensation, don't get into irrelevancies, and don't badmouth anyone. You should be able to cover all of that in ten to fifteen minutes, and you don't need to worry that you're giving the candidate too much to remember. You might spend a little longer on prep if it's a really complex role or a rookie candidate, but even then, be careful not to overdo it. Any additional guidance you give them can't be at the expense of them forgetting the critical elements we've discussed in this chapter.

Once you've got this down, and you see your candidates coming back to you with great stories about how they took charge, asked the right questions, and sold the employer on why they were the perfect choice, your confidence in this strategy will increase. And then maybe you can start to relax a little when your candidates are heading to their interview.

Maybe. . . .

# Photos – A Life in Recruitment

WBP Founders: Jack Downing, Tom Wieder, the author,
Dave Sanders, and Mike Gionta

**Early years at my recruiting desk**

**My predecessor, Les Zanotti**

**WBP Partners Gala celebrating our 50th anniversary**

Presentation in Venice, Italy 2008

Career Achievement
Award

The author and his father with FBI Director, J. Edgar Hoover (1972)

*Salve amicus es?*

# Chapter 28

# Debriefing the Candidate After the Interview

"How did the meeting go?"

This is the $64,000-question that recruiters wait anxiously to ask from the moment the candidate walk into the interview.

But the success or failure of the interview is only one detail. Debriefing a candidate after the interview is an opportunity to gather a lot of valuable information that will help you handle the next steps.

This doesn't have to be a long, drawn-out affair. Just like the interview prep, five to ten minutes is usually plenty. But try to get in most, if not all, of the following questions:

*How did the meeting go?*

Get this one out of the way quickly. If it went well and they're excited, celebrate with them. If it went badly and they're down about it, commiserate with them and encourage them not to jump to any conclusions yet.

But more importantly, pay keen attention to the flavor of their response.

Most of the time the candidate won't be massively confident or massively discouraged. They'll be somewhere in between. They may even be the kind of person who plays their cards close to their chest and so won't give too much away.

Try to read the tone anyway. When you asked the question, did their enthusiasm rise, or did it fall? Did they say that they got a good vibe from the interviewer? Do they have any criticisms about the process? The volume, enthusiasm, or even hesitation in their voice will tell you a great deal about what they're truly thinking. This initial feedback is paramount.

*Did you get all your questions answered?*

Often, interviews wrap up before a candidate has had the chance to ask everything. This is your opportunity, as their recruiter, to step in, clarify any lingering doubts, or provide additional information. You may even be able to go to the interviewer and get the extra information on their behalf, which most candidates will really appreciate.

*What questions did the interviewer ask you?*

This is pure market intelligence, my friend, absolute catnip, especially if this is your first candidate to interview with a particular client. This intel provides a crystal-clear understanding of the opportunity and the client's priorities, allowing you to better prep future individuals you send to this employer.

*Did you discuss compensation?*

Their answer should always be no. In fact, if you've drilled this into them strongly enough in the prep that they should never do this, and they gave in and had the discussion with the employer, they might even fib to you.

So, if they say no and you sense hesitation, push them a bit:

*Are you sure? It's okay if you did, it's an easy mistake to make when you're under pressure. But I need to know because if go to the employer now to negotiate and they say that you've already discussed it, I'm going to look like an idiot but, more importantly, I can't negotiate on your behalf.*

If they admit to making this error, find out precisely what was discussed. It sucks when this happens, but you need to at least know what happened exactly so you can go into negotiations with the right information.

*From what you learned in the interview, does this sound like an opportunity you'd like to pursue?*

This is the critical question that many recruiters shy away from. But it's utterly essential. If you detect any hesitation, any doubt creeping into their voice, this is the precise moment to deploy the Takeaway Close:

*It sounds as though this opportunity isn't quite the right fit for you. I don't want to waste your valuable time, or the employer's. I'll simply let them know you're no longer interested in pursuing it.*

The natural human reaction is to want what is being taken away. So, if they don't immediately push back and affirm their interest, you've correctly identified that this is *never* going to happen. And you just saved yourself a tremendous amount of wasted effort.

*Did you tell the interviewer you're interested in pursuing the opportunity? And if so, what about the next steps?*

If things have gone really well, you want that direct confirmation of their commitment, and an understanding of what the employer's expectations are for the next step.

## I Don't Know How to Say This, But . . .

A candidate gave me the impression that the interview had gone really well, so I called the employer, full of expectation. And this is what I got:

> "Todd, the candidate . . . well, they're a bit too robust for this client-facing role, if you catch my drift."

> "Not sure I do, buddy. What are you saying?"

> "Todd, this guy must weigh three hundred and fifty pounds!"

I've also had conversations that went totally the other way . . .

> "Todd, have you actually met this lady in person? She's absolutely stunning. She made me so flustered I couldn't even interview her properly."

Is this unprofessional?

You bet.

Are employers human beings who get emotional sometimes and say things they shouldn't?

Absolutely.

So, when this happens, it's our job to navigate this swamp. Because these folks often don't understand the nuances of hiring—especially the legal ramifications of what they're saying. But if you've created a relationship, they are more relaxed to share things better left unsaid.

First of all, when an employer gives you feedback that's, frankly, discriminatory or completely irrelevant to the job, like a candidate's weight or appearance, you never go back to the candidate and tell them that. I'd never bust someone that way. That would be humiliating, and it's not our place to deliver that kind of crushing blow. You convey the message delicately:

> *They liked your qualifications, but they found somebody they liked a little bit better.*

You're not lying outright; you're just omitting a detail that could hurt them personally or open up your client to a lawsuit.

Employers, God bless 'em, violate more EEOC rules than anybody else. They ask things like how old candidates are or if they're married. When you hear these things, whether it's direct questions about a candidate or unsolicited comments like the ones we just discussed, your role is to subtly educate them. You might say:

> *Ms. Employer, you know, you can't ask me that question.*

Or, if it's a comment about their appearance, you simply acknowledge the qualifications and steer the conversation back to what truly matters for the role (if the discrimination is extreme, based on something like race or religion, you will likely want to reconsider working with that client entirely, or at the very least speak to your client's direct supervisor).

Our job isn't to be cops, and if someone doesn't want to hire someone because they're, say, morbidly obese and it's a client-facing role, there's not much point in trying to argue. But we can at least maintain professionalism by reminding them of their legal responsibilities when it comes to their questions and comments during the hiring process. And we can also protect the feelings of our candidates.

There's no reason in the world we should ever let the bad practices and unprofessionalism of an employer (or a candidate, for that matter) blow back on us. You don't need to jeopardize the entire relationship, but you also cannot endorse or facilitate discriminatory practices.

## Keep It Professional

At this stage in the process, you have a lot of power and influence on what happens next. But some recruiters just miss the point entirely. What some recruiters do—and this is absolutely true—is start spinning yarns about how keen everyone is.

They'll say to the candidate:

> *I don't know what you did at that interview, but the employer absolutely loves you. They can't wait to meet with you again.*

And then they'll say to the employer:

> *Hey, I don't know what you did at that interview, but the candidate absolutely loves you. They can't wait to meet with you again.*

The recruiter here is seeing themselves as some kind of romantic matchmaker, thinking if they just tell two people that they secretly have a crush on each other, magic will happen. They're trying to engineer a match, to push people together just to get a deal across the finish line.

But let me tell it to you straight:

> *This is a terrible move, a colossal mistake, and it undermines everything we stand for in this profession.*

First off, it is fundamentally dishonest. Your reputation is the only thing you truly own in this business. You simply cannot afford to play fast and loose with the truth. If you tell a candidate that an employer is interested when they are not, or vice versa, and that truth comes out—and it usually does, believe me—you've destroyed your relationship. People trust you to be truthful and to give them all the facts, the good and the bad.

Second, and perhaps even more critically, this tactic directly contradicts the core philosophy of how a truly effective recruiter operates. You've probably noticed by now that my approach is to put what appears to be a good match together and then spend the rest of the time trying to pull it apart. That's what the Takeaway Close is all about. If I can blow up a placement, early in the process, with a simple suggestion that we shut it down, then it was never meant to be, and I've saved everyone a lot of hassle. I can move on to find a candidate or an employer that is a better fit.

Recruitment isn't about finding a candidate and an employer and trying to force them together. It's about finding a candidate and an employer and figuring out if they are *genuinely* compatible. If they are, and you can see that clearly, then move heaven and earth to make it happen. Except that, if the match is right, aside from a little refereeing, you probably won't have to push that hard.

You cannot, and should not, force a deal. If a placement is going to be made, if the candidate and employer are truly going to "fall in love and get married," it will mostly happen naturally. Our job is to facilitate that, to make the introductions, and to figure out the needs of both sides, but ultimately the decision is theirs.

And with this boneheaded strategy previously mentioned, even if you win . . . you lose.

So, when you debrief your candidate and ask the right questions, aim to determine genuine interest. If it's not there, protect your time and move swiftly on to opportunities or candidates where it is. Learning to spot those subtle red flags early on will save you immeasurable frustration down the road, and the debriefing is a key moment to figure this out.

# Chapter 29

# Determining Urgency

In this game, where we're working on a contingency basis, we're often the only idiots in the room. We're working for free unless a placement gets made. Employers simply do not think twice about wasting our time.

And who can blame them?

They've got pressure and stress of their own to deal with, so when we come in and offer to work on their problem for free, what busy exec is going to say no to that?

But that doesn't mean we have to put up with anything that gets thrown our way. It's down to us to protect our time and, as far as possible, to avoid wasting our efforts. This is why understanding an employer's true level of urgency is paramount. You need to determine if an opportunity is genuinely worth your valuable time and effort.

We've touched on this already in multiple chapters, but it's worth covering it again in more detail because it's one of your most powerful strategies for maximizing your ratio of placements to hours spent working. I want you to read this chapter and lodge in your brain this concept of *urgency*. Your goals should be to assess this with employers, directly or indirectly, at every possible stage.

The base question that helps with this is:

*What have you done to help yourself thus far?*

This applies to both the candidate and the employer, although in this chapter we'll be focusing more on the employer side of negotiations. Their answer, or lack thereof, speaks volumes. But there are also signs that will help you deepen your assessment.

Look out for these signs, and if they're present, dig deeper to find out whether they're significant to this question of urgency:

## 1. How long has the position been open?

If the position has been open for just a couple of weeks, they likely haven't had the chance to truly vet internal candidates or other avenues. You can take the job order, sure, but be cautious about investing significant planning and recruiting efforts right away.

If it's been open for six months or more, you've got a much bigger problem. This indicates serious issues. They might have unrealistic expectations about compensation or qualifications. Or perhaps, there's just a sheer lack of motivation on their end to hire. In this scenario, you must dig deeper to find out what's causing the holdup.

## 2. What is the cost to the company of not having this role filled?

This question can be a good way to justify your "above average" fee and can even develop urgency in the mind of the employer where it may not have properly existed before.

## 3. What kind of candidate flow are they currently receiving?

If they tell you they are working with multiple recruiters who charge a low fee, say, 20 percent, they need to understand that those recruiters are not actively recruiting. They are just mining their candidate database and they're not doing any heavy lifting. In fact, this may explain why the employer has not been able to fill the role. The quality of candidates is not there.

In this kind of scenario, you're in a strong position to explain why their current approach isn't working and that you can solve their problem if they agree to your fee and call off the other recruiters.

## 4. Is the employer considering internal candidates?

If some internal candidates are still being looked at seriously, or if an offer has already been extended to someone, do not engage in a full search. You are likely wasting your time. Wait until that situation is fully resolved before you commit to a candidate search.

What all these considerations have in common is that you're using them to assess whether the urgency is real, because the role has been open for a long time or because it's an important role. If it's the former, is the difficulty in filling the role due to the employer's poor strategy or lackadaisical approach, and if so, are they willing to change their attitude to allow you to do your job properly? If it's the latter, is the employer willing to engage you in a manner that reflects this level of urgency, for example, hiring you under the terms of a Priority Search (see Chapter Twenty-Five)?

To test the employer's urgency and cooperation, you must slice and dice the process. You can do this by asking about their normal hiring process and comparing it to their last hire. What is the typical timeline? What actually happened last time? There is often a significant difference.

Once you've got this information clear, break down every single step of the hiring process and get explicit commitments. For instance, if you present a candidate tomorrow, will they give you feedback within twenty-four hours? How quickly can an interview be scheduled? Will they agree to blocking out specific interview time slots for the candidates you're going to send to them?

If at any point they fail to uphold their commitments, or if you sense hesitation or lack of cooperation, the Takeaway Close will point the way:

> *Look, Mr. Employer, you told me this was urgent, but we haven't received feedback in the agreed-upon time. I'll assume this position is no longer a priority, and I will be removing my candidate from consideration.*

If the employer has a genuine reason for not responding as agreed, such as sickness or a family emergency, then it's fine to give them some slack. But don't swallow bogus excuses, such as "the company has put a temporary hold on new hires." That may be true, but what stopped the client from calling you and telling you this? Be reasonable, but don't be a pushover.

New recruiters often fall into the trap of working on anything that comes their way because they are desperate for activity. But an experienced recruiter, who has learned by being burned at every stage at one time or another, actively looks for reasons not to work with someone and identifies red flags early on.

Work long enough in this profession, and you'll learn this through sweat, blood, and bitter tears. Or you can take it from one who has been there and do this right from the outset.

Assess the level of urgency, investigate it to confirm your conclusions, and then negotiate the terms of service with the employer to see if they'll play ball. If not, have the guts to protect your time by walking away and hunting for better opportunities.

# Chapter 30

# Operating Efficiently and Controlling Your Day

"Didn't we already talk about this in Chapter Sixteen? The old man's losing it, right?"

Wrong.

Yes, I know we already covered this earlier, but how many weeks or months is it since you've studied that chapter? Did you apply all of it? Did you fully develop all those habits? Yes?

Great. But have you kept up to it? Or have old habits snuck in? Is LinkedIn always open in a tab of your browser? How many times a day are you checking and replying to emails? How long do you spend drinking coffee and chatting to colleagues before you pick up the phone and make that first call of the day?

I know how this works. We set great intentions for ourselves, and we start off as regimented as a Navy Seal. But then little distractions start creeping in, like weeds pushing their way through the concrete. We tolerate one or two. And before long, our carefully crafted routine is littered with little time-wasters that add up to an hour or two a day of inefficiency.

Think of this chapter as a gentle kick in the rear. A reminder to review your routine and look for distractions that might be derailing your success.

A few months before I started writing this book, I hired a two-tour United States Marine. He's one tough individual, a real badass. He came in talking about how much money he wanted to make and how he was going to crush the leaderboard. And yet he was on the phone maybe three hours out of a seven-and-a-half-hour day.

I sat down with him and asked him straight: "What are you doing the other four and a half hours?"

But I already knew the answer, even if he didn't. He was bouncing. He'd look at LinkedIn, then check his email, then maybe do a bit of research, and then make a call, probably hitting voicemail. Then he'd do it all over again—look up the next person, review their background, make another call, and it's another voicemail. This is incredibly inefficient.

The answer is to compartmentalize. Remember, this is like a workout. When you go to the gym, you don't lift weights for ten minutes, then swim for ten, then play racquetball for ten, then stretch for ten, and then go back to lifting. You do all your lifting at one time, all your swimming at one time, all your stretching at one time, and then you cool down. That's efficient.

It's the same on your desk. Block out specific times for specific activities. From 9:00 to 11:00 a.m., that's prime-time phone time for marketing calls. From 1:00 to 3:30 p.m., that's prime-time recruiting. And then you have dedicated blocks for administrative tasks like returning calls, sending emails, sending fee agreements, updating the database, and planning for tomorrow. You don't mix them up. You don't bounce.

I know, I know. I already told you this, but it's all too easy to forget and slip back into bad habits. You need to be tough with yourself. Because every time you decide to reply to an email during prime telephone time (this one's really important—it's an exception), you're weakening your resolve, and it'll keep happening.

Look at Seth, one of my junior partners. Seth made $400,000 last year. Why? Because he's efficient. He starts working at 5:00 a.m., doing all his administrative stuff, so that when he comes in, he can be on the phone all day long. That's a habit that becomes a routine.

Be like Seth. Come in every day, operate like a well-oiled machine, and crush it.

## Telephones Are for Dinosaurs

I know for a fact that there are some new, young recruiters who are reading this and thinking they can figure out a better way.

"Why are we using phones when we've got email and social media and AI? I can automate all of this."

Well go ahead and try it if you must, but I guarantee you'll run into the same problem over and over.

You can't establish a meaningful relationship with another human if you don't *talk* to them.

There is no technological alternative to a real conversation between two people, because technology is always a limiter between two people's ability to connect, unless you're doing nothing but video calls. But given that the goal is fifteen conversations a day, it would be very hard to schedule and conduct that many video calls.

If you want to be pedantic, even the telephone is, to some extent, a restrictive technology. Talking to someone in person, in real life, is always the best option when possible. When it isn't, a phone call (or video call) is the next best thing. Anything beyond this is going to produce poorer results, virtually by definition.

Technology, whether it's LinkedIn or email or AI, is a tool, a helper. It helps you cut down on the number of cold calls you have to make by better targeting the right people, sure, but it cannot replace the human element. You have to talk to people, you have to build rapport, and you have to build trust. My son, Marcus, who has recruited lawyers for the past thirteen or so years, uses texting for quick information, but he has to talk to them.

People often reach out to me, calling me their "friend who happens to be a recruiter," or words to that effect, and will still call to ask about career changes, even after I've been off the desk for twenty years. Do you think that would happen if my principal communication method with them had been via WhatsApp messages?

Telephones might be for dinosaurs, but I'll bet you good money that it's the "dinosaur" recruiters that will always have the best, long-term careers in recruitment.

# Chapter 31

# Increase Your Chances of Recruiting Passive Candidates

Todd:　　Good morning, Mr. Passive. This is Todd Dawson, calling from Omaha, Nebraska. I'm a recruiter specializing in placing dog food sales professionals. We've not spoken before, but I wanted to introduce myself to you personally and confidentially. Do you have a few moments to chat?

Mr. Passive: Hey, Todd. I appreciate you reaching out, but I'm quite content in my current role. I am not really interested in exploring any new opportunities.

Todd:　　Hey, that's great. Good for you. You wouldn't believe how many sob stories I hear every day from people who hate their boss, aren't getting paid enough, hate the commute. It's great to talk to someone who's in a good place. Would you go so far as to say you're in your dream job?

Mr. Passive: (chuckles) Well, I wouldn't go that far.

Todd:　　Gotcha. You know, I make dozens of calls every day, and I talk to a lot of people in your business. I often come across truly remarkable opportunities that are not publicly advertised. I'd hate to call you in, say, sixty or ninety days, only to tell you about a position I just filled, and you then tell me you wished I had called you about *that* opportunity. So, I gotta ask . . . if I had that once-in-a-lifetime, that diamond-in-a-coal-mine opportunity, would you want me to call you about it?

Mr. Passive: Well, sure. Who would say no to a dream job? But it would have to be something really special.

Todd:  Of course. So, what would that look like for you? What would make you sit up and take notice?

Mr. Passive: I don't know. Maybe a million bucks a year for working one day a week.

Todd:  (laughs) Hey, if I find that job, I'm not coming to you, I'm taking it for myself. But let me put it like this: Where do you genuinely see your career in five, ten, even twenty years? What kind of long-term aspirations do you have?

Mr. Passive: Well, ultimately, between you and me, I can see myself in a VP role, maybe even Senior VP.

Todd:  Nice. And are you on track for that where you are now?

Mr. Passive: You know, I'm not sure. For a while it looked like it. But there's been a lot of restructuring here over the last few years, so it's hard to say.

Todd:  Ah, I see. Well, that's a great place to start. So, for instance, if I stumbled on a role that had a clear promotion track, would that be one to call you about?

Mr. Passive: Oh, sure. I'd definitely take a look.

Todd:  Gotcha. Now, given your aspiration to move toward leadership roles, are there any companies you would particularly love to join? And, conversely, are there any companies you would absolutely not consider working for?

Mr. Passive: Hmm, that's a good question. I hadn't thought about it quite like that. There are a few companies I admire, for sure. I'd have to think about it. And, to be frank, I'd want to involve my spouse in any career moves, so I should probably talk to them.

Todd:   I hear you. I've been married for *X* years, and I would do exactly the same.

Mr. Passive: So, do you have any roles at the moment like that?

Todd:   Good question. But I don't want to waste your time by presenting an opportunity that is not truly aligned with your aspirations. Perhaps you could share a bit more of your background with me, so we can determine if we have a match? Right now, I don't know if you're a quarterback or a wide receiver, if you understand my meaning.

[End scene]

This would be the moment when I'd pull out a fresh Candidate Data Sheet and start filling it in. Mr. Passive is now a great addition to my database of prospects and on their way to becoming a warm associate.

There are very, very few people who are so happy in their current role they wouldn't at least consider the opportunity to move into a new position that would further their career. It's simply a matter of getting to know them and finding out what motivates them and where their ambitions lie.

If you speak to a new candidate and they don't show interest initially, don't conclude the call unless they explicitly insist the conversation is over. Instead, pivot to the "dream job" question which, you may have noticed, is effective in many different scenarios. And if they don't have a good answer to this, dig into their mid-term and long-term career goals. Candidates who aren't interested in a sideways role may be very interested in a role that would represent a promotion.

Even if you never wind up placing this person, the way you conduct this first contact can result in a genuine rapport and a relationship that leads to other opportunities with other firms and other candidates. On top of that, the way you handle the conversation may present an opportunity for more searches to work on when *this* person is making hiring decisions.

Every person you speak to in your target industry, unless they are totally unwilling to have even a short conversation, has value. And, if you're doing your job correctly, you can potentially be of great value to them as well.

# Chapter 32

# Marketing a Candidate – What Do You Say When They Say No?

Clients have a million different ways to say no, but in the end it doesn't matter what their objection is. If you've been granted the gift of connecting with someone in person, instead of being shunted to voicemail, you're going to milk that call for all its worth.

When you're marketing a candidate to an employer, and they say no, always treat this as an opening for a conversation. Unless it's a very aggressive *"NO!* I'm not going to talk to you,"* there are always ways to pivot.

What you don't want to do is get into an argument.

If someone says no to hearing about your candidate, don't waste time trying to convince them that they're wrong. In the client's mind, if they don't have a vacancy or they have a freeze on hiring, it doesn't matter what you're selling. They're not buying. Trying to convince them otherwise just makes you an irritating mosquito.

Instead, aim to open up the conversation into a broader discussion.

An inexperienced recruiter will feel deflated when the employer they had high hopes for rejects their candidate out of hand, so they ask something like:

*Do you know anyone who might be interested in this candidate?*

No employer in the history of the world has ever replied positively to this question. Because even if they do know someone, there's no incentive for them to put time and brain power into figuring out who that is. They're not going to do your job for you.

So, the recruiter newbie gets another no and has little choice but to end the call.

A seasoned recruiter, however, doesn't even blink when they get a no. To the professional, a no indicates that the call is just getting started.

## Every Call Has Value

We've already talked about how to get the most out of every conversation (see Chapter Twenty), and a little later, we'll dig deeper into how to flip a call. For now we'll just cover the basics of turning a rejection into a meaningful conversation.

Always remember that you're only talking to a limited number of people each day, so you simply must squeeze as much juice as you possibly can from every single conversation.

Here's how you do it: When an employer tells you they are not interested in your candidate, your marketing call is over. So, you pivot instead to a recruiting call, where you can explore other potential opportunities for yourself and identify new leads:

*That's okay, I appreciate you at least taking my call. But before I let you go, you know, I specialize in placing professionals in this industry at many levels. I'd hate to speak to you in the future and tell you about a position I just filled and hear you say, 'Gee, I wish you'd have called me about that.' So my question is, if I find an unbelievable opportunity, a diamond in a coal mine, a once-in-a-lifetime career opportunity, would you want me to call you about it?*

Most will respond positively to this, in which case you use the technique we covered in the previous chapter. Ask them what that opportunity would look like, ask them about their long-term ambitions, and so on.

You now have another great candidate (albeit passive) in your database, and the next time you call this person, they're almost guaranteed to take your call. When they don't know if you're going to pitch them another candidate or present them with a dream opportunity, they're not going to dodge your call.

## Movement in the Marketplace

Once you've recruited this person, keep the conversation going. If they'll let you, try to extract all the knowledge out of their head about their industry, their company, and what's happening in the marketplace that you might not yet know about. Who's interviewing? Who's moving? Who's thinking about moving? Who's expanding into a new territory? These are all breadcrumbs you can follow to unearth new opportunities.

Here's a nonexhaustive list of questions. It's always better if this information can be teased out organically, rather than the person feeling interrogated. But until you're confident in your abilities in this area, feel free to keep this list around to remind you of the topics you want to get into:

- When was the last time your company hired someone? Where did they come from? What was that person hired to do?

- Did you have multiple qualified candidates to pick from? Who finished second, third, and why?

- Did you make any offers that were not accepted or lost to a counteroffer?

- How long were you looking to fill that position?

- When was the last time your company had someone resign or was terminated?

- Was there someone you hated to see leave your organization? Who was it? Where did they go?

- Did you replace that person? How did you identify the replacement? Where did they come from?

- Are there any other departments/divisions in your company that need quality candidates?  What can you tell me about that role? Whom should I contact to learn more?

- Does your company/division have any growth plans where you might need a quality candidate or two in the next six to twelve months?

- Is there any type of hard-to-find candidate I could present to you who you would want me to contact you about now or in the future?

- Who's the best up-and-comer in your industry?

- Who is the best person you know doing what you do?

## There's Always Room for a Superstar

Sometimes hiring managers will get a little snippy and try to cut you off from calling in the future. They'll say something like, "Why are you calling me about a candidate when I don't have a vacancy?"

What they're trying to do is discourage you from calling again. They want it to be a "Don't call me, I'll call you," kind of relationship.

When you sense this is happening, try my Kansas City Chiefs illustration:

> *I hear you, but you know, even a business with a full roster will usually want to know when a superstar becomes available. It's like when Kansas City was winning all those Super Bowls, but they still broke the bank to sign Chris Jones, because he was one of the best, if not the best, defensive tackle in the NFL. Even with a stacked roster, do you not think you could find a place for a superstar? The best in the business don't come on the market very often, so I'm guessing that if they become available, you'll at least want to know. Is that fair?*

## "Just One More Thing . . ."

Whenever Peter Falk in the role of Detective Lieutenant Columbo says those words, you know something amazing is going to happen. And, of course, it rarely stops at "one more thing." But there's a good lesson for us. Because at some point you're going to sense the person on the other end of the phone has run out of time, patience, or both, and is trying to get you off the call.

Maybe they'll even be blunt about it:

> *Look, I'm sorry, but I don't have time for all these questions.*

You now have a balancing act to perform. You don't want to end the call before you have enough to have made the interaction worthwhile. But you also don't want to annoy the other person to the extent that they'll never take your calls again. So, channel your inner, scruffy detective:

> *Sure, look, I know your time is really valuable. I just have one more question for you.*

Most people, unless they're genuinely running late for a meeting, can spare you two more minutes. Especially if you are providing value, asking compelling questions, and, perhaps most importantly, showing yourself to be a fun, interesting person to chat with. Trust me, the better you get at making pals with the people you speak with, the less likely it is they'll try to end the call.

Ultimately, you only need to be mildly more entertaining than their work, so this really shouldn't be that difficult.

# Chapter 33

# Marketing a Candidate – What Do You Say When They Say Yes?

It's ironic that we spend all this time on phone calls trying to get a yes, and then when we do we immediately become suspicious.

Well, that's what we're supposed to do. We already identified this situation as a classic trapdoor (Chapters Nine, Ten) where the employer says yes they'd like to hear more about our candidate, and then we blow it by immediately firing off a bunch of selling points.

Most of the time, when we make this mistake, one of two things happens: Either what we just said doesn't precisely match what the employer wants so they end the call, or it matches perfectly and, because we don't have a contract in place, they reach out to the candidate directly and cut us out.

That's two really good reasons to take a careful pause when someone says yes. It's a good position to be in, but before we do anything else we need to establish whether the employer is genuine in their interest and, if so, whether they're actually going to be a good match.

I have two really good responses to a yes, and you should use whichever one you feel most comfortable with:

1. *I'm glad you're interested in learning more about my candidate. Are you actually recruiting for this position at the moment?*

2. *I'd love to tell you more about the candidate, but first maybe you could share some information with me about what you're looking for so we can determine if we have a match.*

If the employer is genuine, they'll be more than happy to talk more. And it's straightforward to probe a bit and determine if there is a genuine opening or if this just a tire-kicking exercise. Ask the usual array of questions around what problems they have that your candidate can solve, what they have done to help themselves thus far, the level of urgency for the position, how long it's been open, and so on.

What you're doing with the cautious approach is controlling the call, gathering the necessary intelligence, and separating the serious calls from those that will lead nowhere.

## Too Eager?

It sounds odd to be concerned when an employer seems too keen, but not when you understand human nature. Most businesspeople instinctively understand that it's always wise to play your cards close to your chest. The more interested, and excited, they are by the sound of your amazing candidate, the more likely they are to feign indifference. They'll ask for more details, but they won't let on that you've really piqued their interest.

So, when someone gives you an enthused *yes!*—or they quickly move to a discussion about money—you're absolutely correct to see this as a red flag. They're probably fishing for information to find out what's happening in the market, who's moving, and what salary expectations are.

You don't want to let on that you're suspicious. Sometimes you just come across someone who wears their heart on their sleeve or doesn't have a poker face, and you don't want to come across as rude or cynical.

But you also don't want to have your time wasted.

In this scenario, treat their interest as genuine, but ask questions that cut to the chase:

"My candidate has a really bright future, so it's important to find the best place for my candidate. Can you give me, say, three reasons why they should quit their current position to join your company?"

A tire-kicker will either try to wrest back control of the conversation, or they'll serve up banal responses such as: *We're a great company*, or: *We're the number two company in the Midwest*. By contrast, a genuinely interested person will feel compelled to come up with something concrete, so you take them seriously.

> *The last two people we hired in similar roles were promoted within twelve months.*

> *We're about to launch a new product, XYZ, that sounds like it will fit really well with your candidate's experience.*

If they don't give really specific answers to your questions, push harder. Ask the employer to give you real examples and anecdotes you can take to your candidate. If they still hold back, you can then jump to the conclusion with a Takeaway Close:

*Thank you for sharing, but it doesn't sound like there's enough there to really get my candidate's attention. If you think of anything else that might change their mind, please let me know.*

## Protect Your Candidate

If the conversation goes well and the employer has the potential to be a good fit for your candidate, you can then present your candidate officially, but you must do this correctly. Don't be pressured into giving away any specifics about your candidate until you have a clear understanding of the position and, ideally, a signed fee agreement in place.

This isn't just about protecting your business and your commission, or some bureaucratic formality.

*It's also your responsibility to protect the candidate's confidentiality.*

Your candidate, in all likelihood, is currently employed, and their current job could very well be jeopardized if their name is thrown around indiscriminately.

You must—*must*—shield them from that unnecessary, premature exposure.

And don't be afraid of grumpy or flaky employers. By upholding strict confidentiality, you not only safeguard your candidate's career but also demonstrate your unwavering professionalism. You're showing yourself to be an honest, ethical, trustworthy recruiter. And in this industry you can't buy that kind of reputation.

If the employer pushes for the candidate's name before you're ready, or implies you don't truly have a candidate (*You're just fishing for a job*), stand your ground. For example:

> *I understand why you might think that. We both know there are many recruiters who operate that way. But my approach is quite different. I never fish for job orders. Frankly, I have job orders coming out of my ears. My business model is built on identifying truly exceptional candidates—what I call the* needle in the haystack—*those who are motivated, interested, and possess a marketable skill with a great track record. So, my goal in talking to you today is to find the right haystack for that needle. I'm also a fierce advocate for my candidates. Which is why I never share their name without first ensuring there is a genuine match and that I have their express permission to proceed.*

Feel free to express this in your own words. In fact, it'll sound better if you do. This isn't some clever line or sales tactic. It should reflect what you actually believe. Finding the right role for your candidate and protecting their interests should be instinctual. If it is, then you won't ever be pressured into revealing your candidate before the time is right.

# Chapter 34

# Candidate Red Flags

Once upon a time, a recruiter found an amazing candidate with just one shortfall: He'd been in his current job for only a year.

When asked why he was so keen to move after such a short time in this role, the candidate said he'd received promises about development and promotion fast-tracking that hadn't materialized. Not only that, his family also wasn't happy in the area they lived and wanted to move. And the commute was killing him.

In short, he wanted out of there as soon as possible.

The recruiter, thrilled at landing such an experienced, motivated candidate, worked night and day to find a new role. He soon found an employer that represented a great fit for the candidate. The area was good, the commute was half the length, and the manager he would be working under had a great track record of helping his people move up the ladder in record time. The salary was the same as the current role, but with all the other benefits, this was still an excellent opportunity.

The candidate attended the interview, performed well, and received an offer a few weeks later. At which point the candidate took the offer to his existing boss and used it as leverage to get him to come good on the failed promises, along with a 10 percent pay bump.

You see, it turned out that the candidate had no interest in moving and was just using the recruiter and the employer to get a counteroffer. The complaints about the family and the commute were just half-truths to cover his real intentions.

The recruiter was very sad and wanted to go to the candidate's house to throw down, but an older recruiter told him this was a bad idea and that, besides, the whole thing was really his own fault for being naive enough to believe that candidates always tell the truth.

Most recruiters will eventually experience something like the above. It happens, and sometimes there's no way to predict it. But most of the time there are red flags that, if we're smart enough not to ignore, will tip us off that working with this particular candidate is, at best, a colossal waste of time.

In the opening example, being in the current role for only a year was a red flag. But if the candidate told me that he wanted to move because of failed promises, my first response would have been:

*Have you spoken to your employer about your frustrations? What did they say? And, if not, why don't you make an appointment to speak to them and air your concerns?*

We want what's best for our candidates, right? Well, in some cases, the best thing for them is to stay right where they are.

If the candidate is fundamentally dishonest and is trying to use me to get a counteroffer, they might continue to lie. But the more they have to lie to me, the more likely I am to pick up on it and figure out that something isn't adding up.

It comes back to my favorite technique in virtually every scenario. Ask questions. Lots of questions. And listen carefully to the answers.

If something doesn't feel right, then take a pass.

With employers, we're looking for urgency and cooperation. Those are the roles that are the easiest to fill and have a high percentage chance of success. Similarly, with candidates, we're looking for motivation, commitment, cooperation, and honesty. Those are the people who are easiest to place and, again, have a high percentage chance of success.

Be ruthless in this regard. If you only take on really solid roles and candidates, yes, you might lose out on the occasional placement, but your completion rate is going to be sky-high. And you won't have to suffer the frustration of wasting time on fruitless searches.

Over time, you'll get a feel for when a candidate is not quite as they're presenting. Until your radar is tuned in, however, look out for these ten red flags:

## 1. Short Tenure

If a candidate has been in their position for less than a year, as we've just discussed, this needs checking into. The candidate needs to have a truly compelling reason to leave because employers are 100 percent going to query this. Employers, understandably, want to see stability. The days of most employees staying in place for ten to twenty years are gone, but even so, there is an expectation that the candidates you present will have been in their current role for at least three years.

Press them on this, directly and thoroughly, and only take them on if they have a really compelling and believable reason for needing to move. And, ideally, their role immediately before their current one should be a long tenure.

## 2. Too Many Job Changes

Three job changes in four years? This is even worse than the previous red flag, and even if the candidate has a really good reason for wanting to move, you should probably still pass. Most employers are not going to touch someone with this level of instability and are not going to care how good their excuse is.

This is a good example of a scenario in which you should be encouraging the candidate to try to solve their current problems in a way that doesn't require them to change jobs. For the sake of their long-term career, they need to tough it out and add some solidity to their resume.

## 3. Refusal to Provide Professional References

Refusal to provide references is less of a red flag and more of a giant flashing light with accompanying klaxon.

I appreciate that the warnings in the chapter seem really obvious, but it's amazing how well candidates can spin yarns to justify the warning signs and convince recruiters to ignore their instincts. If you're an agreeable person generally, it can be hard to get used to saying no to people. But you've got to thicken up that skin and protect your time.

A red flag can only be defeated by asking lots of questions, getting really good, reasonable, honest answers, *and* a confidence that these problems are not going to put employers off.

Anything less, and you shouldn't feel in the least bit guilty for advising the candidate to either stay put or find a different recruiter.

## 4. Unrealistic Expectations

When a candidate has outlandish expectations, particularly in the area of compensation, this can easily come back to bite you later. Deal with it now by bringing the candidate back to reality. Ask the candidate how much the last pay raise from their current employer was. Probably more around 3, 5, or 7 percent. If, for instance, they say they want a role with a 20 percent pay bump, you can explain why the percentage from their current employer is more realistic. You might be able to get them 10 percent, but this is where you hammer down the candidate's expectations. Understand that many candidates feel once they have a recruiter involved they can get a bigger bump in salary. You must explain reality to them *now*.

You need to be really sure that you've convinced the candidate to adjust their expectations. Because if you get them an offer at 10 percent and then they dig their heels in and demand 20 percent, it makes you look bad and unprepared to the employer and can easily derail the entire deal.

If a candidate is really deluded and says they're looking for a 50 percent bump, don't even try to reason with them. Their judgment is in question, and you'll almost certainly run into even more red flags with this person further down the line.

## 5. Compensation Changes Mid-Process

This is a tremendous red flag. If a candidate provides one compensation target at the outset and then changes it later, especially when an offer is imminent, this means they weren't being truthful. It makes the candidate look bad, and it makes you look bad by association.

There's always debate over whether recruiters should favor candidates or employers when it comes to disputes. My view is that, while we try to be evenhanded, at the end of the day, it's the employer who pays our fee. I wouldn't be comfortable trying to convince a client to take on a candidate once they've shown themselves to be untrustworthy. If they've lied about this, what else have they lied about?

When this red flag is raised, I either kill the deal or jump straight to a Takeaway Close:

> *We agreed that 10 percent was a reasonable target at the outset, so it's a problem that you're now insisting on 20 percent. I'm going to go to the employer and tell them that there's no deal to be had here, and I'm withdrawing you as a candidate.*

If the candidate backs down, all well and good. But if they don't object, then you and the employer have dodged a bullet. You can, with a clear conscience, cut your losses on this project and let the candidate go.

## 6. Family Isn't Involved

As you're aware, we're not allowed to ask a candidate about their marital status, but we can ask if there is anyone else who will be involved in the decision to change jobs. If you then discover the candidate has a spouse or partner who works locally and high school–aged children, and this role change is likely to involve relocation, the likelihood of it falling apart is high.

Encourage the candidate to discuss the idea of moving roles with their family and then come back to you. Then listen very carefully to the response. If he says that he discussed it with his family and there was no problem and everyone is onboard, that sounds very much like no conversation actually happened.

Even worse is when the candidate says that it's his decision and that his family trusts him to make the right choice for everyone.

If it sounds like the candidate is being evasive or naive, then that's the time to pass.

None of which is to say that having a family means you shouldn't take on the candidate. But there's a lot of conversation to be had about how the move will affect the family and whether this is going to become a sticking point later on. Ask lots of questions here, and make sure you've fully obliterated the red flag at the start of the relationship before you do any actual work on the project.

## 7. Lack of Action

A candidate claims misery in their current role but hasn't updated their resume. Are they lazy, lacking motivation, or exaggerating their situation?

Whichever is the case, this sounds very much like you've found yourself a tire-kicker.

I'll say it again, because I really want you to absorb this deep into your psyche: Your career as a recruiter will be more enjoyable and more lucrative when you only take on roles and candidates that have clear urgency and are motivated to move forward.

## 8. Working With Multiple Recruiters

Just like an employer, if a candidate is already working with several other recruiters, your chances of making a placement diminish significantly.

## 9. Accepting Counteroffers

Candidates with a history of accepting counteroffers are a very risky endeavor. Working with them is gambling, not just with your time, but with the employers' as well.

This also suggests someone who is motivated primarily by money.

A candidate who is focused on compensation to the exclusion of almost everything else can be a red flag in itself. I hesitate to list it as such because money is always an important factor for candidates. Of course it is. But when the desire to make more income blocks out everything else, including common sense, tread carefully.

## 10. Withholding Information or Lack of Cooperation

I've already explained that when I start working with a candidate, I make it very clear I expect them to follow directions and respond to calls and emails promptly. And that, if they don't, I will take this as a sign that they're no longer interested in working with me.

But you have to follow through on this. If a candidate fails or refuses to provide requested information or doesn't follow through on commitments, let them go. Unless they have an incredibly good reason, such as an injury or a family emergency (though, even then, is a quick text message that hard?) they're showing a lack of cooperation and trustworthiness. That's not good for you and it's not good for the employers you're trying to place them with.

At its core, dealing with red flags is about asking questions. The quality of questions you ask separates a great recruiter from the mindless herd. My background in law enforcement taught me how to interview and ferret out the truth, and one of the primary signs of honesty is when a person's story stays consistent and never changes.

Dig deep until you get the full story. And if at any stage you have doubts, employ a Takeaway Close to confirm your suspicions. Never be afraid to pull apart a deal early in the process. If you can kill a deal early, it never had a chance to begin with. The earlier you do this, the more wasted time and aggravation you avoid.

There is no shortage of candidates. And we get to decide who we work with. Not the other way around.

# Chapter 35

# Employer Red Flags

Once upon a time, a recruiter engaged an amazing client with just one shortfall: They needed the position filled within four weeks.

Apparently, the position had been open for three months, and the chairman was so annoyed, he told the hiring manager that if he didn't fill the seat in four weeks he wasn't getting a bonus that year.

The recruiter, thrilled at landing a high-profile, motivated employer, worked night and day to find three stellar candidates to present to the client.

At that point, the client told him that the chairman had given the role to a family member, so he no longer needed to see the candidates.

The recruiter was very sad and wanted to go to the client's office and throw down, but an older recruiter told him this was a bad idea and that, besides, the whole thing was really his fault for not taking a proper brief and not listening to the advice he'd been giving the recruiter for the last six months. And sweet Jiminy Christmas, he'd better start getting his act together or he was going to wind up needing a recruiter of his own.

Motivated clients are great. But they're also high risk because they're liable to do something unexpected or reactionary. If the recruiter in this scenario had been paying attention—instead of mentally spending the commission on a hot tub before he'd earned it—he'd have followed the advice in Chapter Twenty-Five and engaged the client under a Priority Search arrangement which would have included a nonrefundable deposit.

Employer red flags are very similar to candidate red flags in that they're typically based around motivations, commitment, and crucial information that is being withheld. The only real difference is that, in some instances, you can protect yourself from the uncertainty by asking for that deposit.

In most instances, just as before, you're going to respond to a red flag by taking a sledgehammer to the deal and seeing how easy it is to break it apart. If it crumbles under pressure, you can walk away safe in the knowledge that you just dodged a bullet.

Here are some of the main red flags to watch out for when speaking to employers:

## 1. Unrealistic Expectations

The employer says they need someone with a decade of experience, but they want to pay a salary more appropriate for a rookie. This disconnect is quite common, for all sorts of reasons, but mainly because employers don't know the market like you do. You know— or at least you should know—what the expected salary is for the different positions and levels of experience in your industry. Which makes it your responsibility, as a professional search consultant, to educate them on the realities of the current market.

If they remain rigid in their low salary bands, asserting that is all the budget allows, or that HR won't let them pay more, recognize that it's going to be nigh on impossible to find what they're looking for, and walk away.

## 2. Too Recent or Too Long

If a position has been open for less than two weeks, this might feel like you've won the lottery (and you may have), but it's also a high risk. The employer probably hasn't got their act together in terms of whether they're going to promote internally, speak to candidates from previous interviews, or even dissolve the role entirely.

Take a thorough job order, and if there's even a whisper of a suspicion that they might do something that will push you out of the deal, cut and run. Or, at the very least, maintain some contact for a few weeks until it's fully clear what their approach is going to be and whether they're going to need your services.

Conversely, if a role has remained unfilled for three months or longer, this suggests a profound lack of urgency, potential compensation issues, or deeply unrealistic expectations. The employer might even have other recruiters on the project or an offer already extended. If you take a thorough job order, you'll discover all of these details. And, hey, none of the above might be true, and this might wind up being a job worth taking. But proceed with a healthy degree of skepticism.

## 3. Lack of Urgency

If, while you're taking the job order, the employer isn't able to articulate the reason why filling the position is urgent, or explain the financial consequences of it remaining vacant, this is a distinct red flag. An unfilled position can cost a company significant sums, potentially tens of thousands of dollars each month. So, if you sense a lack of motivation, set down some Takeaway Closes:

> *If I send you three qualified, motivated, and interested candidates within the next forty-eight hours, will you agree to provide me with feedback within twenty-four hours of receipt?*

## 4. Fee Agreement Issues

Some fee pushback or haggling isn't a major problem in itself, but if they're slow returning the fee agreement, or they send it back with the fee or guarantee terms modified independently, challenge them immediately and don't be pushed around.

Pricing integrity is critical. Compromising early on sets a precedent that you're willing to agree to a last-minute change in terms when a deal is ready to go. Your fee is your fee, and if they don't like it, there are plenty of 20 percent resume-shufflers they can hire instead.

If they ask for a discount and are prepared to negotiate reasonably, that's okay. But they must give you something in return, perhaps a reduction from 33 percent to 30 percent if they agree to the removal or reduction of the guarantee period. Or maybe even 25 percent if they agree to use you exclusively in future hiring needs.

## 5. Multiple Recruiters or Candidates in Process

If an employer is engaging with numerous recruiters for the same position or has multiple candidates deep in their hiring process (especially internal candidates or an offer that has already been extended), this is dead on arrival. Your chances of making a placement are microscopic. Follow up with them in a few weeks, just in case everything has fallen apart and they're desperate for a real professional, but this is an easy pass.

## 6. No Commitment to Interview Times

This is the key test of the hiring manager's seriousness and whether their urgency is performative. Pre-assigned interview times are easy to arrange, and they move things forward quickly, so if the employer isn't willing to play ball on this, it's Takeaway Close time.

## 7. Admission of Turned-Down Offers

If an employer informs you that previous candidates have declined their offers, they're either making low-ball offers, or there's something rotten happening in the interview. Dig a bit, but unless there's a really good reason, this one's going nowhere.

This is not an exhaustive list. Eventually you'll develop a sixth sense that tells you whether you've found a legitimate opportunity or a waste of everyone's time. Don't ignore these signals. It can be hard to walk away, but you can't protect your time by taking a punt on every role that passes your desk.

If you find it hard to pass on these opportunities, then make good use of the Takeaway Close to stress test the motivation and commitment of the client. Once you see the client prevaricating or making nonsense excuses, it's much easier to accept that the red flag is real and not paranoia.

And allow yourself to feel good about walking away. You've acted responsibly and saved yourself time that is better spent on real opportunities.

## Stand Your Ground

Around six years into my career, I identified a particularly strong candidate and was making marketing calls on their behalf. I connected with an HR professional, and from the outset, the conversation was extremely combative.

The HR person, without preamble, declared, "I don't know why you're calling me. We don't use recruiters. You people are nothing but a waste of time. I don't have time to speak with you."

To which I replied, "Okay, well, I appreciate you classifying yourself."

She paused, and then asked, "What do you mean?"

"It's simple. There are only two kinds of companies: Those we recruit for, and those we recruit out of. I appreciate you categorizing <company name redacted> for me. I hope you have a fine day."

I ended the call.

Barely ten minutes later, my phone rang again. It was her boss, the Vice President of HR, and he was quite agitated.

"I understand you just threatened one of my HR people."

I countered, "Sir, I do not believe I did that."

"You just threatened her that you were going to recruit out of us!"

"No, that is not what I said. I thanked her for categorizing <company name redacted>. There are only two kinds of companies: Those who we recruit from and those who we recruit for. That's not a threat. That's just a plain explanation of how recruitment works. You can do what you will with that information."

A little while later, I placed that very capable candidate. With a competitor of <company name redacted>.

Do I recommend getting into arguments with grumpy HR people? No. And maybe I wasn't doing myself any favors by responding in kind. Today, I would probably handle that quite differently. But what I will say is that, as a recruiter, you're going to speak to a lot of assertive, antagonistic people who are going to try to push you around.

Don't let them.

You don't have to be rude or belligerent. But you also don't have to put up with being insulted. We all know that the recruitment industry has, many times, given itself a poor reputation, but you're the exception. You're a professional who helps businesses grow through great recruitment and helps candidates advance their career through great opportunities.

Have confidence in your methods and your value. And the courage to outline reality to people, even if it is uncomfortable for them.

# Chapter 36

# The Thirty-One Steps of the Recruiting Process

What do recruiters and NBA professionals have in common?

People think they both get huge fees just for doing a couple of hours of work.

From the outside, looking in, it appears that professional basketball players play a few games a week and spend the rest of the time kicking back by the pool. But if you were to look behind the scenes, you'd see the half dozen training sessions a week, the workouts, the ice baths, team meetings, physical therapy, nutrition planning, media obligations, community outreach, and endless hours of travel.

Likewise with recruiters. From the outside the employers just see the emails introducing them to the candidates, and then the invoice when the placement is done. They don't see the hours of phone calls and emails and research and candidate prep and reference checks and networking.

You could say that this doesn't really matter, but this misconception can sometimes come up when people query the fees we charge, either when the fee agreement is being drawn up, or even after the placement is made and the invoice has been received. This can happen especially if we manage to match an available candidate with an employer within just two days of taking the assignment. I suppose it's not too surprising that some will balk at a bill for tens of thousands of dollars for a process that only took a few days.

On the one hand, you could argue that we shouldn't have to justify our fees. But if we must, we can say that we're not being paid by the hour, we're being paid to solve a problem. And if we do it in days, rather than months, isn't that to our credit? We've saved the employer potentially tens of thousands of dollars by not leaving them shorthanded.

You should absolutely explain it like this to any client who questions your fees.

Another approach I like to use is to remind the employer that, while the process of finding them a candidate may have only taken a few days, this doesn't take into account the hundreds or even thousands of hours spent beforehand on phone calls and emails to build our network in the first place. If they'd prefer to pay by the hour for that, they're more than welcome to do so.

But it's going to cost a heck of a lot more than 30 percent.

If the client really pushes, especially if they're trying to compare you with recruiters who charge a lot less, the final step is to draw a clear distinction between what a recruiter who charges a 20 percent fee and a what recruiter who charges a 33 percent fee actually does.

A low-rent recruiter maintains a database of candidates and, when given a brief, they send their best matches to the employer. This is very different from a high-level recruiter who finds a candidate to order, especially when it involves recruiting someone who is already in another role that they're happy in.

That would be like comparing Lebron James with someone who plays a pickup game a couple of times a month.

It's an entirely different league.

A while ago, I broke down my recruiting process into thirty-one steps. So, when someone pushes really hard on fees and clearly doesn't appreciate how much time and effort goes into our work, I share it with them.

Feel free to do the same:

1.  Take a complete job order.

2.  Make a recruiting plan.

3.  Conduct file search.

4.  Gather names.

5.  Contact potential candidate.

6.  Profile potential candidate.

7.  Check references.

8.  Present position to candidate.

9.  Present candidate to employer.

10. Set up first interview.

11. Prep candidate for first interview.

12. Prep employer for first interview.

13. Debrief the candidate from first interview.

14. Debrief the employer from first interview.

15.  Set up second interview.

16.  Prep candidate for second interview.

17.  Prep employer for second interview.

18.  Confirm second interview with both parties.

19.  Debrief candidate after second interview.

20.  Debrief employer after second interview.

21.  Conduct closing/negotiate.

22.  Offer/Accept/Establish start date.

23.  Prep resignation.

24.  Debrief resignation.

25.  Celebrate.

26.  Prep billing.

27.  Fill out billing paperwork.

28.  Stay in touch with the candidate until start date.

29.  Confirm that the candidate has started.

30.  Stay in touch with the candidate and new employer.

31.  Invoice the client.

# Chapter 37

# The Ten Most Common Composition Mistakes on Resumes

I can count on the fingers of one hand the number of times I've received a perfect resume from a candidate.

They're frequently terrible, occasionally passable, and rarely useable without at least some changes. So, it's your job, if you have a candidate you want to present, to tell them how to make their resume more effective.

The reason resumes are so often unusable is that they tend to be created for a world that no longer exists. Once upon a time, an employer might get a dozen resumes and they would study them all for hours to decide who deserves an interview. These days, the employer gets two hundred resumes, and they first get sent to a bored HR person whose job it is to whittle the pile down to a dozen. In practice, this means the HR person isn't looking for good resumes; they're looking at each one and scanning it quickly to try to find a reason to ditch it.

A candidate's resume, on its own, isn't going to land them a job. But it can sure as beans get them rejected before they've even got a foot in the door.

There are entire books about how to write a resume, but no one has time for that. So, here are the main things to look out for that either need taking out or changing:

## 1. Photograph on the Resume

Unless a job explicitly requests it, which is pretty rare, there's no need for a photograph. It could raise discrimination anxiety in the mind of the employer. And, hate to say it, but is it that hard to imagine that an HR person with no skin in the game might ditch a resume because they don't like your candidate's face?

## 2. Grammatical Errors and Spelling Mistakes

This one is obvious. A resume doesn't need to be perfect, but if it's riddled with typos, this immediately signals a lack of attention to detail and professionalism. If a candidate is content sending out a sloppy document, an employer will reasonably assume that same level of sloppiness will translate directly into their work.

## 3. Overly Specific Objective Statement

Many candidates like to include an objective statement, such as a desire for a leadership position or a C-level role. Ambition is great, but this approach can inadvertently restrict a candidate's opportunities. They are, in essence, putting a box around themselves in the mind of the reader. It's far more effective to allow the resume's content to speak for itself regarding the candidate's aspirations.

## 4. Focusing on Daily Duties Instead of Accomplishments

This will be a problem with virtually every resume you see. Resumes will meticulously list every task the candidate performs as if there's some kind of bonus point for having a busy job. Most people understand the basic functions of common positions, so this information is redundant and just winds up making the resume way too long—one page should be the goal, two at a push.

When you spot this, tell the candidate to swap out duties for achievements and contributions. Did they save the company money? Did they complete a project ahead of schedule? Did they increase revenue or efficiency? Did they win an award? These are the nuggets that make a resume stand out as well as make it more interesting to read than a dry to-do list.

## 5. Including Personal Information

Personal details, such as a candidate's fraternity affiliation, hobbies, height, weight, age, race, or religion, have no place on a professional resume. They're irrelevant to the candidate's professional qualifications and should be left off entirely. Their spell as a linebacker in college might make for a fun detail in the interview if the employer turns out to be a football fan, but it's not appropriate or helpful on a resume.

## 6. Interests and Hobbies

If there's a direct, demonstrable connection to the role (a keen artist applying for a graphic design job, for instance) there might be an argument to include it. But otherwise, for similar reasons to the above entry, it has no place on a professional resume. Employers don't care about a candidate's passion for skydiving if they're applying for an actuary position. These details are best saved for an interview, when more rapport has been established.

## 7. References

Many candidates still include a line stating "References available upon request" or even list references directly on their resume. This should be a given so doesn't carry any weight. The appropriate time to discuss references is when an employer specifically requests them, typically later in the process.

## 8. Endless Narratives

Employers want to see at first glance that a candidate is strong. If the resume is pages long, the important details will get lost in the noise. Or, worse, the employer might mistakenly assume that the candidate has a ridiculously long resume because they're a job hopper. Refer back to Item #4 on this list (see above), *Focusing on Daily Duties Instead of Accomplishments.* This should be the meat of the resume, and achievements can be summarized easily without losing their impact.

And as a sidenote, do not offer explanations for gaps in employment unless specifically asked.

## 9. False or Negative Information

Any claim on a resume—an inflated degree, current employment status, or exaggerated salary history—can be verified. If you spot something and you can forgive it as an honest mistake, just get them to correct it. Otherwise, you should reconsider representing the candidate entirely.

Equally, candidates must never include anything negative on a resume, even if it's true. Especially if this comes in the form of criticizing a previous employer.

## 10. "Flair" or Unusual Formatting

Fluorescent colors, unconventional fonts, or distracting symbols make the resume stand out . . . as one to be dropped in the trash. The resume should be on plain, white paper and printed in a standard font. The only thing that should stand out are the qualifications and accomplishments. For the same reason, watch out for personal website links and unprofessional email addresses (love2party@email.com).

When you advise a candidate that they need to make changes to their resume and they push back, gently remind them that you do this for a living and that you know which resumes are most likely to make it to the interview stage and which ones are more likely to get dropped in the trash.

> *To be frank, Mr. Candidate, you've got a great chance of landing this role, but this resume is going to hurt that chance.*

You don't need to micromanage the small stuff. If they're absolutely insistent that they include a line about their love for mountain biking, it's not the end of the world. The most crucial elements are brevity (one or two pages) and achievements over duties.

Nail those two parts, and you can be confident that your candidate will land in the "qualified and interested" pile.

# Chapter 38

# Why Candidates Need to Avoid Counteroffers

Pop quiz.

Your star candidate gets a job offer and hands in his notice with his current employer. The employer wants to have a meeting about it, so your candidate calls you and asks what they should do. Even though you've already coached them on how to handle this scenario.

Do you say:

1. *Don't take the meeting. They'll try to make a counteroffer; it's a trap.*
2. *Take the meeting and, if they make a counteroffer, tell them to stick it.*
3. *Take the meeting, hear what they have to say, and politely decline any counteroffer.*

The correct answer is, of course, going to be revealed at the end of the chapter.

But whatever you think the right response should be, we can all agree that we should be thanking our lucky stars that the candidate called us first. Because accepting a counteroffer is almost always a terrible idea.

Which is why my advice on this subject is: Once your candidate decides to accept a new job offer, have another serious conversation with them about why they should expect a counteroffer and how to handle it.

The first thing your candidate will tell you is that this isn't anything to worry about because their employer never makes counteroffers. This is almost always wrong. Nearly every employer, unless they're flat broke or were going to fire the candidate anyway, will make some kind of counteroffer. They just don't advertise this because otherwise everyone could pretend to have a job offer elsewhere just to get a salary bump.

Explain to the candidate that, even if they're right, they should be prepared for this scenario all the same. Because they're a stellar employee, the employer is probably going to panic about how they're going to cope without them and how hard it's going to be to find their replacement and will try to get them to change their mind somehow.

Your job now is to explain to the candidate again why accepting a counteroffer is a bad idea.

## Remind the Candidate of Their Why

No matter what you say to the candidate, if they get a counteroffer that offers them more money than the new job, they're going to be tempted. So, remind the candidate of all the reasons they're moving which have nothing to do with finances.

It could be: the opportunity to move back to their home town, cutting the commute time in half, a clear promotion track, or more time to spend at home, playing football with little Billy. If you took a proper brief in the first place, you should have no problem giving them a bunch of reasons why they shouldn't be swayed by dollar signs.

But what if there are no Whys, and the reason for moving is purely the money? Well, that's one of the reasons a candidate motivated purely by their bank balance is a red flag candidate (see Chapter Thirty-Four). If it's "all about the Benjamins," they're a prime risk for being won over by a counteroffer. In this situation, your best approach is to ask the candidate if threatening to leave is the only way to get the promotion and pay bump they deserve, is this really the best place for them?

## Discuss the Negative Consequences

It's no great surprise that a high percentage of people who accept a counteroffer end up leaving their position within the next few months. Once you've accepted a job offer elsewhere, a line has been crossed that the employer won't forget. It will always be at the back of their mind that their star employee isn't happy and could leave at any time. Maybe they start quietly looking for a replacement or taking more calls from recruiters with candidates to pitch.

Unfortunately, even if you can convince a candidate of this, they will still be vulnerable to a counteroffer. It's hard to leave a job and colleagues behind, especially if they've been there a long while. If the counteroffer is juicy enough, the candidate's common sense might just fly out the window.

A smart way to protect them from this situation is to role-play the resignation conversation. Once the candidate has accepted a new job offer, schedule some time together as soon as possible and practice what they're going to say to their boss. This can be a time-consuming and sometimes emotional process, but it's effective.

Walk them through the precise words they should use:

> *I've enjoyed working with this company and appreciate the opportunity I've been presented here, but the time has come for me to take on my next challenge.*
>
> *I've given my word to my new employer to accept their position, and I'm excited about this new chapter in my life. So, while I appreciate the thought, I won't entertain any counteroffer.*

Instruct them to be firm, to show resolve, and, as much as possible, to take the emotion out of the situation. They must never volunteer negative reasons for leaving or say anything derogatory about their current employer or colleagues. They're ready for a new challenge, and this opportunity is too good to pass up.

## Warn the Client About Counteroffers

The only good thing about prospective counteroffers is that they give us good leverage to ensure our client makes our candidate a really solid and attractive offer.

When negotiating, tell the employer plainly that, because the candidate is so valued, a counteroffer is inevitable. Encourage your client to anticipate this situation and consider making an offer that is "unreachable" by the current employer.

This is good for the candidate because they get the best possible offer. It's good for the client because they're more likely to have their offer accepted.

When carrying out the roleplay, if you sense hesitancy or weakness on the part of the candidate, don't let this slide. No one wants to be on the end of an "I've accepted a counteroffer" call.

If you've asked all the appropriate questions, you can remind the candidate again why they've decided to make this move and why staying is in no one's best interest.

If necessary, use the Takeaway Close to press the candidate one way or the other:

> *Listen, my friend, if you don't want to pursue this opportunity, it's okay. I can get you out of it as quickly as I brought you in.*

Let's do the pop quiz again and see if your response has changed now that you've read this chapter.

Your star candidate gets a job offer and hands in his notice with his current employer. The employer wants to have a meeting about it, so your candidate calls you and asks what they should do.

Do you say:

1.  *Don't take the meeting. They'll try to make a counteroffer; it's a trap.*
2.  *Take the meeting and, if they make a counteroffer, tell them to stick it.*
3.  *Take the meeting, hear what they have to say, and politely decline any counteroffer.*

Don't go with 1. It's impolite, and if possible, you don't want the candidate to leave under a cloud. If the candidate is so vulnerable to a counteroffer that you don't even want them to hear it, you've already messed up somewhere.

Number 2 works, but it's not ideal. Again, you want your candidate's exit to be smooth, professional, and have minimal drama.

I'm sure you figured this out. Number 3 is the correct response. It's professional, it makes the candidate's position clear, and if you've prepped them correctly then you have no reason to fear that they'll cave in.

## The Nuclear Option

What do you do if the candidate comes back to you and says they've accepted a counteroffer?

First of all, don't panic. Most counteroffer agreements are verbal and are not binding. You still have a window to fix this.

Remind them of the reasons they wanted a move in the first place.

Remind them that counteroffers are usually just a holding solution while the employer hunts for their replacement.

Remind them to ask themselves if it takes the threat of leaving to get what they deserve, is their employer really seeing their true value?

Even if they've said yes to a counteroffer, they can still go back to their employer and say, after further consideration, that they've decided that moving on is the best decision.

Another good angle to take is to position accepting a counteroffer as losing control of their career.

> *When you decided to seek a new opportunity, you took control. Accepting a counteroffer surrenders that control back to your employer, putting you on the defensive. You'll spend the next year or two wondering if your boss is ultimately going to try to replace you.*

*Are you going to take control, or are you going to surrender your career?*

In a worst-case scenario, where the counteroffer—at least in the mind of the candidate—is too good to turn down, and you can't convince them to see sense, there's no reason you shouldn't approach your client, explain the situation, and invite them to submit their own counteroffer.

This isn't ideal and should be a last resort. The client might feel like they're being played, and you don't want to damage your relationship with them. But if you know the client trusts you to be upfront with them, it's worth a try.

One of my recruiters experienced this a few years back. The candidate was on $135,000 but was happy to move for the same money for personal reasons. Their employer made a counteroffer of $155,000, which the candidate felt was too high to turn down, even if their long-term future ended up being elsewhere.

My recruiter explained the situation to the client and suggested they make a counteroffer of their own, but to make it their best shot because they probably wouldn't get another one. They agreed and came back with an eye-watering $175,000 offer, which the candidate gladly accepted.

The candidate went from $135,000 to $175,000, and my recruiter was excited because the counter to the counter worked in their favor for a change. It doesn't happen very often, but it *does* happen.

It doesn't often work out this well, so don't see this as a strategy. But it well illustrates that if you're unfortunate enough to get a candidate accepting a counteroffer, it doesn't mean the deal is dead.

# Chapter 39

# Learn to Say No

There are some cultures where saying no to a client is considered the height of stupidity. The idea is that you always say yes and then figure it out later. Business leaders love to tell the likely exaggerated story of Bill Gates agreeing to build an operating system for IBM, even though he'd never done it before. In my view, there's no credit in bluffing your way into a job.

I would argue, for various reasons, that this is a bad idea in business. For starters, giving the impression that you know how to do something that you've never done is deceptive. But it's an even worse idea in recruitment.

Always remember, the only person who is truly going to protect your time is you. Candidates and employers won't think twice about consuming your time. And if you cede control of your time, you'll wind up with fifty hours a week of busywork trying to place terrible candidates with worse employers.

*We say no to low-grade opportunities today, so we can say yes to the golden opportunity tomorrow.*

We already covered red flags in Chapters Thirty and Thirty-One, so you should already have a good idea of when a no is the right response. But here's a quick reminder:

## Candidate Red Flags

- Short tenure in current role

- Too many job changes

- Refusal to provide references

- Previously accepted a counteroffer

- Unrealistic compensation expectations

- Lack of motivation or cooperation

- Family not on board with relocation

- Working with multiple recruiters

- Undisclosed information or dishonesty

## Employer Red Flags

- Unrealistic urgency or expectations

- Unrealistic compensation

- Refusal to commit to a fair fee

- Existing Internal Candidates or Offers

- Working with one of more other recruiters

Now I want you to roleplay each of these red flag moments in your head and practice saying no. You don't need to be unpleasant or rude, just gently explain that this isn't the right fit and send them on their way.

I want you to practice this because if you come from a culture where yes is the default response, you're going to have to condition yourself to cut out that nonsense. If you don't, I promise you that at some point, you'll look around your desk and realize that you're working your fingers to the bone on opportunities that have a less than 10 percent chance of turning into positive outcomes.

So, practice saying no and learn to say it confidently. And if it feels like you're saying no far more often than yes, rejoice because this means you're on track to becoming a highly productive recruiter.

Now, having said all of that, let me tell you about POEJOs.

## The Serendipity Deal

The POEJO acronym was created by the MRI recruiting network many years ago, and it stands for *Presentation On Existing Job Order*.

It's not particularly descriptive, but it has always stuck in my mind. It's the label for a candidate you've either previously said no to, or who you would usually say no to but unexpectedly represents a potential fit for a role.

In other words, a candidate you don't want to spend time marketing might have an unlikely match materialize. There's no harm in presenting them to the employer with appropriate caveats.

For instance, let's say you're talking to a candidate and there are red flags. They've job-hopped a bit, and their salary expectations are a little on the high side. You definitely don't want to spend time marketing this person. But then you remember a role that, for whatever reason, you've been struggling to fill for a number of weeks. And, you know, take out the red flags, and this person would be potentially a fit.

You tell the candidate about the role and they get really excited. It's an area of the industry they're really interested in, and they're even willing to come down a bit in their salary expectations.

Congratulations, you've just landed yourself a POEJO!

The next step is to call up the employer and be upfront with them. Tell them about the red flags, but then also tell them why this individual might be worth a look, especially given how challenging it's proving to find a perfect match.

Realistically, a match is still unlikely, but because the time you're investing is minimal, there's virtually no downside. You're not going to actively market this candidate, but making the introduction is quick and easy, and every now and again you'll land a match and make an easy sale.

This works in reverse as well.

You could be talking to an employer, and there are red flags popping up all over the place. The position has been vacant for months, they can't pay above market rates, and they've started exploring promoting from within. This is an easy no. You're not going to spend days, or even weeks, searching for great candidates who are probably just going to pass anyway.

But then you remember that candidate you spoke to last week. She had a criminal record, so you decided to pass, but she's really keen on a move back to her hometown, and hey, it just so happens that this employer is in that very location.

> *Well, Mr. Employer, I'll be honest, I don't think this is a role I'm going to be able to work on. However, it just so happens I spoke to a candidate last week who really wants a move to your location. She's got the experience and she's motivated, but the only snag is that she had a DUI five years ago. Is that a dealbreaker for you, or given how much trouble you're having filling the role, is she worth a look? Yes, she's told me that she's been a teetotaler ever since. But I suggest having an honest conversation with her to see if this is something you can overlook.*

If the employer is open to it, you agree to terms and then make the introduction.

And that's it.

You're not taking on either the candidate or the employer as a full client. You're not spending significant time on this. But a little voice is telling you that this could be an unlikely match for both of them.

Don't ignore red flags, ever. But keep track of your no's, because sometimes you'll spot a potential match among the rejections that can result in a quick and easy win. And I tell you—those can be some of the most enjoyable placements you'll ever make.

## I Don't Talk to HR

I make it a practice not to speak ill of individuals. But I have no problem giving my frank opinion on the general role of HR in recruitment.

I really don't like to work with HR unless it's absolutely necessary and I'm forced to!

Why? Because, more often than not, they just get in the way. When they're tasked with taking the point on hiring, it seems like their primary goal is to cut the recruiter out.

I get it. They want as much power as they can grab onto because that's how they keep their job, but in my opinion, they should be handling benefit information and employment verification. They have no business—none—selecting talent.

Frankly, they don't know how to do it. They convince themselves that they can run a radio spot, post an ad on Indeed, attract a metric ton of resumes, and then, after spending days dropping most of them in the trash, pick a handful of middle-of-the-road candidates because the resumes have the keywords they're looking for. You can try to tell them that the best candidates are already in good roles and not hanging around job boards, but they won't listen. Most of the time all they see is your 30 percent fee and then convince themselves (and more senior people who should know better) that they can do it faster and cheaper.

It's almost comical how arrogant that is.

Talent acquisition is what we do for a living. And we know, all too well, that great placements do not come from resume shuffling.

So, when a hiring authority attempts to send me to HR, this is a HUGE red flag. I push back, firmly but professionally, and insist on working directly with the hiring authority.

If they insist, then I go to the Takeaway Close:

> *Look, I'll be honest with you, I cannot work with HR. In my experience, HR has a habit of wiping out perfectly qualified candidates simply because they don't like how a resume reads. That's a waste of everyone's time, especially ours. I'm happy to loop them in on our progress, but if I have to go through them first, I'm not going to recruit on this position.*

I know a *lot* of recruiters don't have any issue with working with HR. And that's fine. It's their choice. But I want feedback from the actual decision maker, not an intermediary who just tells me their company isn't interested in the candidate and doesn't provide me any other information or feedback. Give me the decision maker every time.

I encourage you to take the same stance. But if you want to test it out one time and see for yourself, good luck.

# Chapter 40

# Case Study – Protected Status

It was a late night in the office. Most of the other recruiters had gone home. The lights were dimmed, and the only sound was the distant hum of the Dyson as the cleaner tidied the office.

Our recruiter—let's call him Frank—was finishing up the notes on a failed placement. A sharp and experienced member of my staff, he'd poured time and effort into a search for an engineering firm in Omaha. He'd sourced, vetted, and presented a qualified engineer. No corner-cutting and no puffing. Frank had run a solid campaign.

But despite his best efforts, Frank couldn't get the employer to meet the final terms of the agreement. The relationship was amiable enough on the surface, but once it came time to talk numbers, the cracks started to appear.

After much back and forth, Frank recognized that an acceptable agreement just wasn't going to happen. He made the call and terminated the active recruiting relationship for that specific search. Fair enough, right? Business is business.

But then Frank's email inbox pinged.

It had only been thirty minutes since he'd had the telephone conversation with the employer to explain his decision. And while the discussion had been a little tense, both parties had acted professionally.

Until now. . . .

Frank opened the email with a little trepidation. He didn't want to have to go another round with the employer. Now that a decision had been made, he wanted to move on to other, more fruitful opportunities.

But it was worse than that.

> *Hi Frank,*
>
> *We're disappointed that we weren't able to come to an agreement on terms for your candidate, but we accept your decision to terminate our active recruiting relationship.*
>
> *However, we must emphasize a critical point regarding our engagement moving forward. As you know, we have a signed fee agreement in place with your firm. We look for long-term relationships, and we believe that, considering we are signed up with you, **you will stay away from approaching our people**.*
>
> *Our firm expects to be granted **"protected status."** We are fortunate to have some very good and longtime associates with little turnover, and we trust that our mutual understanding, established by our signed agreement, provides this protection, precluding your firm from recruiting any of our employees.*
>
> *Sincerely,*
>
> *[Employer's Name]*

Frank did his best to keep a straight face but was unable to stifle a chuckle. He hit Reply and thought for a few minutes about how best to respond. In the end, he decided on this message:

*Hi* [Employer's Name],

*No.*

*Sincerely,*

*Frank*

## Something for Nothing

I'll be honest and admit I used a little artistic license in the above story. Frank's response was much more professional than I've implied.

But, my oh my, that's the email I would have been tempted to respond with.

The employer, in this instance—and this isn't at all uncommon—had a fundamental misunderstanding of how recruitment works. Instead of politely asking that we don't recruit from them, they outright *demanded* "protected status." They presumed that, merely because a fee agreement had been signed, that this somehow meant our firm was now barred from ever approaching any of *their* employees.

They were dead wrong.

Protected status is something we only provide to our clients, as a courtesy, *when they hire someone we recruit for them and pay the agreed fee.* Shouldn't this be obvious? We can't pay our bills with fee agreements. There has to be a mutual benefit.

Essentially, the employer in this scenario is trying to get something for nothing. They want the benefit, the protected status, without fulfilling their end of the bargain. They hadn't hired a single person we referred and hadn't paid us a dime in fees.

Frank had terminated the relationship because they were engaging in classic tire-kicking behaviors. They had what they said was an "urgent need," but really they just wanted to see a bunch of resumes from highly experienced engineers that we'd recruited for them, and then switch up the job parameters, haggle over the fee, and try to get a new hire on the cheap.

And when that didn't work out for them, they thought a signed fee agreement was enough to stop us from recruiting their people.

Here's the plain truth you need to drill into your brain as a recruiter:

*Protected status is earned, not assumed.*

You must never, ever, provide protected status to an employer unless they've actually hired a candidate you've referred to them and paid you your fee. And that privilege—and it is a privilege— only remains as long as they continue to engage you. Once your relationship with the employer ends, the protected status ends with it. Sure, if they've been a long-term client, you might leave the shield in place for a time, but that's purely at your discretion, or that of your firm.

But it's always best to try to avoid this kind of foolish misunderstanding if we can. If you're working with an employer who looks to be, potentially, a long-term client, it's a good idea to explain the nuances of protected status to the company *before* you begin a search.

Lay it out for them:

*Once you hire someone we've referred to you, you gain protected status for one year after that hire.*

This sets out the expectation clearly and professionally, and if the employer asks further questions about how they can secure that protection for longer, this is a good sign because it shows they're serious about doing business and having a long-term relationship. You can then talk about how continuing to hire through you will keep the protected status in place.

But if things go south, don't be afraid to stand your ground. Your value, your worth, is determined by your expertise and your ability to deliver solutions, not by being bullied.

This is one of the great ways in which you can separate yourself from your competition. If you get a reputation for holding firm to your convictions of what you will and will not do, and that you're not for moving, you're less likely to get employers trying to take advantage.

It's the same the other way around. If you get a reputation for wilting under a little pressure, giving in to inferior terms, and slashing your fees, before long everyone will expect a discount.

Frank's story above is a prime example of how to be clear, authoritative, and unwavering in your principles, and how to ensure you chiefly engage with serious, cooperative clients who value your service. You're selling a solution to a problem, not just a warm body to fill a seat.

So, be a rock. Be firm in your convictions. Be like Frank.

# Chapter 41

# How to Handle the Most Common Marketing Objections and Flipping the Call

I've observed over the years that a lot of recruiters love to recruit but hate to market.

That's understandable. People get into this game because they want to make placements and earn fat commissions. When you get a client with an opening, you know for a fact that there's a fee just waiting to be earned as soon as you find the right person. So, what tends to happen is that recruiters start off with good intentions, splitting their time between recruiting and marketing, but once they get a few clients, the marketing goes out the window.

The problem with this is that it's actually *easier* to place a great candidate with a great company than it is to find a candidate for an open role. It might not feel like it because when you're trying to place a candidate, you'll get a lot of rejections. And no one likes that feeling. It's disappointing. Whereas when you're looking for a candidate for a role, you get a lot more positive responses because everyone likes to be recruited, even if they've no real interest in changing jobs.

If you don't believe me, just do the math. There are, obviously, a lot more candidates in the world than there are businesses. So, when you're trying to fill a role, you're searching a very big haystack for a very small needle.

But when you've got a great candidate, you've already found that needle. Now you just need to find a great haystack to place it in. If you've interviewed the candidate thoroughly and confirmed them to be a Most Placeable Candidate (MPC), you're going to find a good home for them. Genuine, high-quality professionals are too rare for most smart companies to pass up.

So, though you might not be wild about it, even when you have some good clients with roles to fill, you should never neglect your marketing. Calling up employers and turning them into connections and, we hope, clients, pays off in both the short-term and the long-term, and it's one of the most effective ways to spend your time.

It's also worth noting that, when you have an MPC in your pocket, getting an employer to give you the time of day is much easier than just calling up to see if they have any roles. It gives you an in, a compelling reason to keep speaking with you. Instead of calling them to ask them to do something for you, you're calling them because you have something you can potentially do for them.

No getting around it, I'm afraid. If you have dreams of one day having so many active clients that you can eventually stop making marketing calls, you need to disabuse yourself of that idea. Marketing will always be a core part of your activities, presuming of course that you actually want to be at or near the top of the sales leaderboard and not hovering around mid-table.

Learn to enjoy those calls. Get interested in what people, especially business owners, in your industry are doing. People love talking about themselves and what they do, so encourage them to do so and pay attention. Tell them to brag about themselves because it's okay to brag to their recruiter, that's the candidate's or client's "spice"! You're getting to meet new people and potentially make new lifelong friends who just so happen to be clients. Reframe it in your head so that marketing isn't a chore, it's an opportunity to have fun, interesting conversations with people and get paid for the privilege.

The only other barrier is getting past those initial objections. And that's just a case of learning the smart responses that help you get your foot in the door.

**"We don't use recruiters"** is a classic response. When you hear this, your first instinct might be to retreat, but resist that urge. Instead, agree with the objection, then ask more questions to get them to open up more. This strategy is effective for almost every kind of roadblock. Instead of arguing against objections, it's usually far more effective to agree with it, empathize, and then move on as if the objection never happened. Keep in mind that most objections are often not even strictly true and are just an attempt to get you to end the call. Don't take them at face value.

Here's my typical response to this objection:

> *Okay. Well, you must have a great process in place to avoid the need for external resources to identify and hire the best available talent. Good for you. What's your secret?*

Listen carefully to the answer and look for common ground that can turn the marketing call into a friendly chat between professionals.

And when the time's right, introduce additional questions:

- *Have you used recruiters in the past?*
- *How satisfied are you with the candidates you've found?*
- *How long did it take to fill your last key role?*

What you're doing is looking for the cracks in their self-sufficiency. Perhaps their HR person found it impossible to fill a particular, critical role, so they *had* to use an external resource that one time. That's good intel. Presumably, the client wants to avoid the situation again. What if you could show them a way to reduce their time to hire, and in a way that saves them money and makes your fee negligible? Would they be open to that conversation?

If there are no cracks to be found and they truly aren't interested in using your services, then Plan B is always to flip the call and identify new potential openings and leads to hunt down:

- *Has your company hired anyone in the past six months? Who did they hire, and where did they come from?*

- *Has anyone left your company recently? Where did they go?*

- *Have you heard of any companies hiring or any people interviewing in the market lately?*

- *Have you been contacted about any opportunities you weren't interested in? If so, who was the employer?*

**"We don't pay fees"** is very similar to the previous objection, so the response can be more or less the same. Acknowledge their statement and then gently probe to get them talking about their process, their challenges, and the *cost* of an unfilled position.

If it turns out that the cost of using a recruiter is a genuine concern, you can encourage them to compare recruiter fees with the cost and business disruption of an unfilled position. A 30 percent fee is inconsequential when compared to hundreds of thousands of dollars in lost productivity.

**"Send me a resume"** sounds like a win, but it's often an objection in disguise. People are often less than forthcoming about their genuine level of interest, unfortunately, so this response can be mere tire-kicking or just a way to end the call:

*Send me the resume and I'll review it later when I've got more time.*

This is the same trapdoor we discussed in Chapter Nine. Don't do it. This is selling blind, without knowing what they truly need, and you risk giving away valuable information without advancing your cause.

But don't say no. Once again we agree with them and then ask more questions:

*I'd love to send you a resume, but before I do, are you actually looking for someone right now? Do you have a current opening?*

If they confirm a need, this is your opportunity to take a complete job order, asking those exhaustive questions about what they're looking for, what they've done to help themselves thus far, and the level of urgency. If they hedge or simply say no, then there's nothing happening here. Move on to flip the call.

**"Tell me more about your candidate"** is another variation of the trapdoor. The employer is signaling interest, but you don't know whether their interest is genuine or casual.

*I'd love to tell you more about my candidate, but maybe you could share some information with me about what you're looking for, so we can determine if we even have a match or not.*

## The Ultimate Flip—Recruiting the Hiring Authority

The most profound way to flip a call is to literally recruit the person you are speaking with, even if they initially say no to your candidate or services.

Once you've exhausted all other avenues for market intel, say something like this:

> *As you know, I specialize in our industry placing professionals at many levels. I understand you don't need my candidate right now, and that's fine. I'll call back in another sixty to ninety days to see how things are developing. You've been very generous with your time, but I have one last question for you. You see, I'd hate to speak to you in the future and tell you about a position I just filled and hear you say to me, "Gee, I wish you'd have called me about that." So, my question is, if I come across an unbelievable opportunity, the diamond in a coal mine, that once-in-a-lifetime career opportunity for you, would you want me to call you about it?*

And, yes, I know I already shared this with you (Chapters Twenty-Five and Twenty-Eight), but I also said that I was going to remind you of this a few more times.

*Because. It. Works.*

The next time you call, that hiring official doesn't know if you're reaching out about a candidate for *their* company or a dream job opportunity for *themselves*, which means they're significantly more likely to take your call.

Keep up with your marketing calls. If you find them tough, just remember that it's simply about asking the right questions. Experiment until you find questions that work for you and that get people to open up. And learn to enjoy it. Be genuinely interested in the people you speak to, who they are, and what they do.

I always say I'd rather be known as a friend who just happens to be a recruiter. When you make marketing calls with that mindset, and you learn to relax and be yourself, that's when you'll really start to see relationships developing and your network growing.

# Chapter 42

# Separate Yourself – Follow Up

You don't have to be a recruiter long before you experience working with great clients and, shall we say, not-so-great clients.

Most of the time, it comes down to bad communication. Or more specifically, a lack of communication. Clients say they're going to deliver the offer by EOD Friday, and it never appears. Clients cancel an interview at the last minute over a conflict they should have been aware of weeks ago. Or, worse, they forget to cancel an interview and the candidate shows up, only to be turned away.

There's only so much you can do to avoid these problems. The only person's actions you can really be fully responsible for is your own. Which is why this chapter is about making sure that *you* are absolutely red-hot when it comes to communication. Recruiters get good and bad clients. But clients also get good and bad recruiters.

Nearly every business owner in existence has had the experience of connecting with a recruiter, only to be let down or even ghosted by them. It's way, way too common. But if you're a strong communicator and you work hard to make sure you always follow up when you say you're going to, that's an easy win. You can make yourself look like a top 1 percent recruiter simply by showing up when you say you're going to, and by delivering what you say you're going to deliver.

I say "simply," but to be fair, consistent communication is tricky when you're running a full-service recruiting desk. You're attempting to tame chaos. There is never enough time, and the constant barrage of calls, emails, and unforeseen situations can easily pull you off your plan. But you've got to find a way to deal with this. Failing to follow up often stems from a lack of discipline and organization. And, sure, mistakes are going to happen. And when they do, be quick to own up to them and apologize. But then revisit your setup to make sure it doesn't happen again.

Modern databases are great for allowing you to set reminders for everything, so if you feel like your communication consistency needs work, get someone to help you make better use of the technology available.

Beyond that, the best communicators in recruitment are the ones who have empathy and view things through the eyes of their candidates. There will be occasions when it may not technically be essential to communicate something, but doing so will ease your candidates' anxiety and make you look like the consummate professional. Even if you don't have any additional feedback or information to provide, a simple contact letting the person know you don't have any additional information or update to provide demonstrates you're paying attention.

Let's walk through a couple of scenarios where diligence in follow-up will make all the difference.

## Scenario 1: The Employer Goes Silent in the Middle of a Process

Imagine your candidate, let's call her Sarah, has been through two interviews over a period of three weeks. Sarah is incredibly interested in the opportunity, and you're feeling good about the fit. Then, suddenly, the employer, Mr. Henderson, goes on vacation to the Bahamas for two weeks.

An inexperienced recruiter might just go dark, assuming Sarah will understand or hoping the situation will resolve itself. That would be a mistake. Sarah, on her end, is probably thinking: *What happened? Did I do something wrong? Are they no longer interested?* This doubt can begin to fester, and in a worst-case scenario, lead to them dropping out.

The proactive recruiter, however, will pick up the phone and call Sarah:

> *Sarah, I just wanted to let you know there is a small delay in the process. It has absolutely nothing to do with you or your candidacy. Mr. Henderson hasn't had a vacation in two years, so he's decided last-minute to go to the Bahamas. He's out of reach for now but he's still very interested. I will keep you posted as soon as he is back and we have an update.*

See how that works? You manage expectations, you alleviate doubt, and you reinforce your commitment to her.

## Scenario 2: Managing the Backup Candidate

An employer tells you that they want to hire Candidate A, but they want to keep Candidate B in reserve, just in case Candidate A doesn't accept the position.

What do most recruiters do? They go dark on Candidate B after the final interview, hoping that Candidate B will simply "get the picture" when they stop calling. This is unprofessional and inconsiderate, but this happens because the recruiter doesn't know how to explain the situation to Candidate B without making them feel like an insurance policy.

The solution is not to bury your head in the sand and ignore the candidate. Instead, find a way to frame the situation honestly, without making the candidate feel less valued.

In this kind of situation, I'd present it something like this:

> *The employer was very impressed with you; they thought you were an outstanding candidate, but there are two of you in competition right now. Full transparency, I think the other guy is ahead of you at the moment, but they're in discussion and anything can happen. I'll be checking in with the employer, so if you have any questions I'm available to you. Just give me a call. But that's where we're at right now. I'll be back in touch with you in a few days with an update.*

The candidate is now informed, has realistic expectations, and feels like they've done the best job that they could. Most importantly, the candidate hasn't been left hanging.

By keeping the candidate warm, they're ready to step in if the first choice doesn't work out. By contrast, if you go dark, they might just move on, and you could wind up placing neither candidate.

The crux of the matter is this:

> *Do what you say you are going to do.*

Maintain your reputation as a professional. It really is that simple. Poor recruiters don't think that way. They don't follow up, they miss appointments, they act unprofessionally, and communication only happens when it's in *their* interests.

I've said repeatedly that your time is valuable, and you must protect it by not taking on low-percentage opportunities. The other benefit of doing this is that you're unlikely to get so overloaded that your communication suffers. You'll still be busy, but you'll have the room to commit to your clients and candidates, and once you say you are going to do something, you'll be able to see it through.

That is how you truly separate yourself and build a reputation that is strong on trust and efficiency.

# Chapter 43

# Cultivating Major Accounts by Separating Yourself From the Competition

When you make your first placement with a new client, it's ultimately not about how good the candidate is or how quickly you managed to find them.

It's about the value you deliver to that employer.

It might sound like I'm splitting hairs, but viewing it in this light will help you change the way you view the work you do and, as a result, make it more valuable to the employer. That's the first step to turning a new account into a major account.

A lot of so-so recruiters make plenty of placements, but their relationship with their clients is very transactional. The client has a role, the recruiter sends some resumes over, and maybe one of them gets hired. There's not much more to it than that.

You, on the other hand, are a different breed of recruiter. You're a problem solver, providing a solution to a real challenge faced by the employer. There was a critical hole in their department, and their existing team was stretched thin doing extra work. But you solved that headache and made their life better.

Isn't that the same thing that the transactional recruiter did? Almost. The difference is that you made sure the client recognized exactly how important your work is and that, the next time they have a talent problem, you're the one who can solve it for them with minimal fuss and maximum professionalism.

Then, and only then, can you begin to cultivate that client into a major account.

Your objective now is to subtly shape your relationship with the client so, instead of being seen as a candidate source, you become a true consultative partner and a trusted advisor. An asset that provides insights and market intelligence the employer simply cannot find on their own. This approach allows you to drive revenue with that new client, potentially on an exclusive basis, through multiple hires or even new projects.

Mastering this is going to take time. If you're a rookie recruiter, sorry to break it to you, but the client is going to figure this out. It'll come across in your limited understanding of industry vocabulary and developments, or simply your lack of confidence and authority in the relationship. Don't worry. This is normal. And you're not going to stay in this position forever. While lesser recruiters work themselves into a pattern of mediocrity, you'll be working on your industry knowledge and your recruitment mastery until your expertise is obvious to everyone you speak to.

It starts by simply acting in a professional manner. Be friendly, but also polite and respectful. Don't use bad language. Ever—even if the employer does. Spend less time selling and more time listening to what the client has to say. But mostly it's about . . . you know this by now . . . say it with me . . .

*Asking the right questions.*

You'll have your standard list by now, I hope, written down or printed out until you have them burned into your brain. But if you're not continually adding to your suite of questions, then you're not paying enough attention to what clients are telling you.

Your conversations with clients (and candidates for that matter) should always be inquisitive. You are trying to learn about hopes, dreams, and desires, not just job requirements. This means asking questions that go beyond the basic candidate data sheet or job order form. You need to develop a feel for the person you are speaking with. This means blending business talk with a personal touch—what I call the *in-and-out conversation*. If someone opens the door to talk about something beyond business, walk right through it. If they mention their love for University of Alabama football, talk about their team. It builds rapport, it builds trust, and it makes you  "their friend who happens to be a recruiter."

It probably goes without saying—but I'll say it anyway—people are far more inclined to share and trust someone they perceive as a friend.

Once you're good at this—which means slipping into friendly conversation without it feeling forced or engineered—you'll notice the shift in the nature of what your clients say to you and the questions they start asking you in return. This signifies that you are now viewed by the client as a consultant, and as someone who has valuable business intelligence that they need.

This might lead, for example, to a discussion about how the client can re-engineer their hiring process. You've placed a couple of candidates with them, but the process was too slow, dragging on for three or four months. You can offer suggestions to compress that timeline, making them more efficient and ensuring the employer doesn't lose the interest of top talent.

You'll also notice this change in how you're perceived because your client will take more interest in the MPCs that you bring to them. Especially if you have a track record of bringing them really great candidates you can demonstrate have been thoroughly vetted.

It makes a huge difference to how you and your candidates are received when you can say:

> *I've followed up with the references for Joe Candidate, and I had a great chat with his former mentor. She said that Joe was, and I'm quoting here, "the most promising sales executive she'd ever worked with."*

How many recruiters do you know who actually contact their candidates' references? I'm guessing not enough.

When you get really good at turning clients into major accounts, you can even start to create new roles out of thin air. I had a client, Chris, who I'd worked with for years. He'd become a good friend, and I'd placed nearly a hundred people with his organization. He was easily 20 percent of my business at the time.

His company launched a new product, but they didn't have a dedicated sales division for it yet. And, serendipitously, I'd recently found a phenomenal candidate who was heading up a telemarketing unit in the same industry. I called up Chris and could have easily just pitched him the candidate.

But I did something else instead:

> *Chris, I have an idea for us to make some money.*

This immediately got his attention.

> *We were talking the other day about your needing to put together a sales team for your new product. I've got an*

*even better idea. Why don't you create a new telemarketing unit? I've found this great candidate, and he'd be the perfect person to lead it.*

Chris loved the idea. He took it upstairs, they interviewed the candidate I recommended, and they hired them. That led to a $21,000 fee for me which, back then, was a significant sum. But the real win? They created an *entire new division* for this person, and I was the one who got to fill *all* the positions below that new hire!

That, my friend, is how you turn a single placement into a whole new line of business. It's about bringing them a solution for generating revenue or solving problems they haven't even considered yet.

But don't be thinking that you can just call up all your clients and pitch the creation of a new department. This kind of project only happens when you've put in the hard work to develop a client into a major account, and proved yourself to be a valuable, trustworthy consultant.

## Build Trust and Relationships

You can't rush this process or force it. Let it happen naturally by asking good questions, listening more than you speak (we have two ears and one mouth for a reason), and making genuine friendships with your clients.

Don't forget the basics. Do what you say you are going to do, consistently and reliably. Make those follow-up calls—whether it's after a presentation, an interview, or just to provide an update. Even if there's no news. No news is, in itself, important news.

I haven't repeated the core philosophy of this entire book for a while, and this is the perfect time.

*It's not about you.*

When you genuinely care about making the lives of your clients and candidates better, and when you share little bits about yourself when appropriate, you build a powerful symbiotic relationship where information flows freely. My best clients became friends, people I still have dinner with, people who even tell me they love me.

Imagine that.

Imagine a business where you work with your customers for so long and develop such a great relationship, that they're comfortable telling you how much they care and appreciate you.

Major accounts come in different sizes and flavors. But, in my experience, what they all have in common is that they're based on a strong, genuine business relationship built on trust and respect. Focus on that, and the rest will follow.

# Chapter 44

# Objections by Companies to Paying Our Full Fee

Imagine you had the great fortune to have a one-to-one consultation with Bill Gates.

At the end of the hour, he hands you a bill for $10,000—which, based on his public speaking fees, is low; in reality it would likely cost you somewhere between $500,000 and $1 million for an hour of his time—and you flip out. Ten thousand dollars? For one hour's work? How can he possibly justify that? You could have watched a business development webinar on LinkedIn for an hour, and it would probably have been free!

This reaction is obviously incredibly stupid. You're not paying for the sixty minutes of conversation. You're paying for access to five decades of extraordinary business experience and wisdom, and if you're smart and follow his advice, you'll recoup the cost of the consultation a hundred times over.

And yet it's amazing how many employers fall into the same warped mindset when it comes to paying us:

> *It only took you three days to find this amazing candidate
> who is going to solve all our business problems. Why should
> I pay you $30,000? That's outrageous.*

We already covered how to handle pushback and challenges on fees in Chapters Twenty-Three and Twenty-Five, but what about when clients try to haggle over the price *after* you've delivered?

It's an awkward one. You might expect my reaction to be a hard-nosed refusal to negotiate after the fact. And you'd be mostly right. They ordered the steak, they ate the steak, so they should absolutely pay for the steak. But it's a little more nuanced than that.

Here are the common examples of how this awkward situation can come about, how to respond to it, and the subtle things you can do at the outset to protect yourself from being taken advantage of by your clients:

**"We knew the candidate prior to your presentation"** is a sneaky one. Because if they already know the candidate, they can argue that you didn't make the primary introduction, and therefore, they don't owe you anything. In fact, I know of at least one employer who has deliberately built their own database of candidates through *informal* conversations with recruiters, precisely so that if they're presented a candidate they can check to see if they already know them and then wheedle out of the fee.

This is, of course, completely out of order. Who cares if they already knew the candidate? They didn't know they were a good fit and available until you did the legwork. So what if the candidate's name was told to them two years ago by some hapless recruiter who didn't know better than to get a fee agreement before telling them the name of their candidate?

But you still have to deal with this if it happens.

The above argument, explained firmly, but a little more gently, may do the trick. But an even better tactic is to spike this gun at the *start* of the search.

All you have to do is ask the client if there are any candidates on their "hands-off list." In other words, candidates they already know about, are already talking to, or have already rejected. If they don't give you the name of the candidate you eventually present (or any names at all), and then try to claim that they already knew this person, you can politely remind them that if this was indeed the case, they should have put them on the "hands-off list" at the start. You've established, in good faith, that the candidate is a good fit and available, and therefore they are obligated to pay the fee.

If the employer is really stubborn on this, you have legal recourse. But your chances of winning will increase exponentially if you have documentation in your database, time and date-stamped, indicating that you asked the client about the "hands-off list" and listed the names they gave you (or recorded that there were no names). Database data is usually admissible in court, so this is a good reminder of how important it is to diligently record the details of every telephone conversation you have.

**"You didn't work very hard to place this person"** has already been covered in earlier chapters, but it's the grumble that is most common, so it's good to be really well prepared for it. Much of the time it's a minor complaint, so you can counter it with some simple arguments along the lines we discussed at the outset.

Here are some examples:

> *Our value is in delivering a solution to your problem. It's not about the time spent; it's about the value the candidate is going to add to your business.*

> *I actually spent thousands of hours building up my network and connections before we started working together. The fee gives you access to those resources.*
>
> *To be fair, if I were to charge for every phone call I made, every piece of market intelligence I gathered, and every conversation I conducted to identify the ideal person, the fee would be considerably higher than this.*

This complaint is often a result of the client being unaware of how much work goes on behind the scenes. So you can minimize how often you have to deal with this kind of thing by taking a really deep job brief and communicating frequently and comprehensively with the client. The more they see you as an expert who is constantly updating them with progress reports, the less likely they are to feel short-changed.

**"We didn't sign the fee agreement, so we don't owe you anything"** is easy to avoid. Just make sure they *actually* sign the agreement before you do a lot of work.

But the client isn't entirely correct here. Although a written agreement is standard business practice, oral agreements can still be enforceable. If you can show notes in your database describing your conversations or emails from the client that make it clear the employer asked you to perform a service that you later fulfilled, you have the basis to at least threaten legal action if they don't behave reasonably.

Still. It's much easier to just make sure you get the agreement signed in the first place.

**"I know we had an agreement at 30 percent, but I need to renegotiate the fee. I'm hoping this is the start of a long-term business relationship and this would really help me out."** If an employer says this, the general rule is to politely decline. You provide a premium service, and you deserve to be compensated accordingly. If you roll over on your fee and word gets out that you've compromised your pricing integrity, you're going to be expected to do this for every client.

However, there are some exceptions.

For example, if the candidate's eventual compensation turns out to be much higher than expected, thus making your fee higher than both of you anticipated, you might consider meeting them halfway. I had a situation once where the client ended up hiring two of the candidates I presented, and they asked for reduced fee as a result. Since I was unexpectedly getting double the commission payments, I didn't mind reducing my second fee a little.

Beware, however, if a client tries to haggle you down after the fact on the promise of much more work in the future. It's usually a fib. If they insist that they have a lot more work for you, suggest an arrangement whereby they pay the regular fee for the first two or more placements, and then a lower fee for every placement after that in the same twelve-month period.

It should, in theory, be much easier to reject pressure to lower your fee *after* you've placed the candidate. But recruitment isn't carried out in theory. And when you're riding high, thinking about the commission you just made, and you're keen to get more work from your new client, it's actually very easy to give in to pressure to drop the fee. Just by a couple of points. Where's the harm?

The harm is that when you do it once, you'll be expected to do it again and again. Take pride in the quality of your work. When you have an agreement and you've held up your end, it's perfectly reasonable to expect the client to do the same.

# Consultative Selling in Context – Simple Rules to Follow to Save Your Time

> Time is the school in which we learn,
> Time is the fire in which we burn.
>
> — Delmore Schwartz
> "Calmly We Walk Through This April's Day"

Most recruiters think if they're working twelve hours a day, steam coming out of their ears as they move frantically from phone calls to emails, to video calls, to networking events, then they're succeeding.

Actually, this can suggest the opposite.

If you feel like you're driving yourself into the ground just to keep up with everything, you're probably mismanaging your time and taking on too many low-grade opportunities.

When you feel like there's never enough hours in the day—and nearly every recruiter hits that point every so often—that's a good time to stop and take stock:

- Are you being too liberal when you say yes? If so, can you be more discerning?

- Are you, even now, working on roles or with candidates you're trying to place that, deep down, you know are never going to happen? If so, can you release them and free up time for the more realistic targets?

- Are you splitting your time effectively between calls and admin, or are you bouncing? If so, can you tighten up your schedule and maintaining stricter focus on one thing at a time?

If you're performing well in all of these areas, the next level of time management is in the process itself. Recruiters, if they're approaching their work correctly, are consultative sellers. Meaning they position themselves as trusted advisors offering tailored solutions, rather than just pushing a product (i.e., a candidate) in a transactional manner. This approach is highly effective, and employers—and candidates, for that matter—can always tell when they're talking to a pushy, hard-sell recruiter, and when they're talking to an active listener who is genuinely interested in finding out what they need.

But consultative selling is more than just an effective method of recruiting. It's also a time-saver in itself. A recruiter who masters this approach will ferret out every last scrap of information from the employer or candidate and use this intel to fulfill the opening precisely. The reason this saves you time is not complicated. If you know exactly what the client needs, you're more likely to deliver the right candidate the first time of asking.

Don't underestimate the level of skill and experience required to become a true expert in this. Asking smart, probing questions is a challenge for all new recruiters, but it's no picnic for the experienced ones. In fact, sometimes "the pros" are worse at this because they get complacent. They hear a few keywords from the client and immediately jump to the conclusion of what's needed.

It feels like a shortcut; however, it's anything but. No matter how much all the conversations you have with clients start to blur together, never forget that every position has its own nuances and its own quirks.

Sometimes it's that one, seemingly innocuous question that delivers unexpected gold. Maybe you discover that one detail about the company's future plans that you know is going to have the right candidates falling over themselves to apply. That's the difference between a good recruiter and a great recruiter. It's being willing to keep digging until you find that nugget and to recognizing it when you see it.

Consultative selling is also a route to widening your talent pool (see Chapter Twenty-Two).

> *Everyone I talk to is already making $100,000. What if I bring you someone making $105,000 or $110,000? Would you still want to talk to them?*

> *What if I find someone with ten years of experience who doesn't have a master's? Would you still want to talk to them?*

This is a timesaver because you can cast a wider net. The employer needs to appreciate you are trying to draw from a larger talent pool.

On the candidate side, you're also going to uncover true motivations and urgency. Keep asking why and keep pressing until you find the true heart of what is needed An inexperienced recruiter may ask the question about motivation and the candidate replies they want a shorter commute. Great motivation, right? But an experienced search consultant digs deeper. The experienced recruiter finds out what the time saved would mean to the candidate and what they would do with that extra time. *That's* the *real* motivation.

Something like this:

> *I just want more time to play with my kids, and the two-hour commute each way is making it impossible.*

> *To be honest, the last person in this role was just so resistant to trying new strategies. It would be great to have someone with a more open mind.*

You don't get those details from surface conversations. You get them by being a consultant, recognizing that you haven't yet uncovered the most critical details, and pushing until you find them.

Nothing in this chapter is new. We've covered all of this in more detail in other chapters. But if time is becoming a challenge—and don't worry, this is normal—then review these strategies and commit to improving your skills in this area.

You can run around like a headless chicken and be successful in placements and commissions. But it isn't a requirement. And in fact, you'll have a much longer, much more fulfilling, and much healthier career in recruitment if you learn how to be more efficient and save your time.

# Chapter 46

# Every Call Has Value

My hope is that, at this stage in your development, you're already becoming comfortable with the idea that every call has value. If that's true of you, give yourself a pat on the back because most recruiters don't think like that. Every call instead gets categorized as either *valuable* or *not valuable*, often while the call is still happening.

I understand why this is commonplace—recruiters tend to rate calls based on whether or not they get a candidate or a client—but what they're actually doing is redefining *success* and *failure*.

A call in which you land a client or a candidate is obviously a success. But a call in which you make a good connection, gain some market intel, or get a lead to follow up is also a success. Failure only happens when you end a call without even trying to get past "We don't have a need" or "I'm not looking at this time."

It might feel like a purely semantic difference, but I assure you it's not. When a recruiter only considers a call valuable if they get a client or a candidate, they quickly give up or make only a half-hearted effort to dig deeper. But if your mindset is geared to the idea that, when someone actually answers the phone, you should milk it for all its worth; then you're operating under the assumption that every call has value.

These habits can become entrenched early. Someone says no or doesn't have an immediate need, and the recruiter thinks: *Well, that's it. On to the next one.* They might ask a few half-hearted questions or fall back on agreeing to send an email instead, but they're not really treating that call as if it has value. They're leaving so much meat on the bone you could serve it up in a fancy restaurant.

We've covered, in multiple chapters now, the different questions you can ask, and the different ways you can steer the conversation to turn a "no call" into a valuable call. I'm not going to rehash all of that here. Instead, I want you to examine your mindset when you get on the phone. What is your goal?

If you're all about making deals, that's okay up to a point. It's good to be focused on profitable outcomes. But you need to temper this with something more holistic. Because otherwise, it becomes very easy to slip into the notion that every call is either "a sale" or "not a sale."

It'll feel counterintuitive, but what I want you to do is push the thoughts of deals and sales to one side and instead think of yourself as a problem solver, a deliverer of solutions, and, most importantly, a ravenous consumer of market intelligence.

What this does is adjust the energy of your calls. You become less pushy. Less single-minded. Less self-absorbed. The conversations become more relaxed. More enjoyable. The people you speak to relish talking to you and won't be in such a rush to get off the phone.

That's when the client opens up and shares more information about their position, their company, their hiring position, their awareness of what other people and other businesses in the market are up to. Then, treat every nugget that you're gifted as equally valuable, because you never know which piece of intel is going to pay off in the long run.

One of my recruiters was once talking to a gentleman who mentioned that if a marketing president position in a small Kansas town ever came up, he would be interested. An average recruiter would dismiss this as a long shot and quickly forget about it. But that recruiter entered this into their database notes, thinking: *Every call has value.* A year later, believe it or not, that very opportunity arose. My recruiter called him back, referencing that specific conversation from a year prior. The candidate was stunned that they had remembered and followed up, but they were both glad the recruiter had. My recruiter got a placement he didn't think would ever exist and earned a substantial fee. And, oh yes, also got a very happy candidate who now viewed them as some kind of wizard. No surprise that he was always willing to take their calls and share with any leads that he came across.

Because here's the thing that you usually only notice over time unless someone who's been in the business for decades tells you about it:

*A-tier candidates tend to associate with other A-tier candidates.*

If you recognize that you're talking to a top-tier professional, put making a friend out of them above trying to recruit them. That one contact may eventually introduce you to multiple, high-level clients and candidates.

It's a paradox in a way. Recruiters live or die on their ability to make placements. But gunning for that placement above all else can often be less profitable. Try pushing this into second place behind becoming a helpful, friendly, generous contact to the people you meet.

Once you understand this, you're playing the long game.

I've seen excellent recruiters who post great numbers year in, year out. But if you look closely, you'll observe that they have to maintain a high-energy, long workday output throughout their career, just to stay in one place. By contrast, my numbers got better over time and, if anything, I was able to work less. I could take a vacation for several weeks, come back to the office refreshed, and still be top of the leaderboard.

How?

The answer is in this chapter. So, if it isn't clear to you by now, re-read it until it is.

**Chapter 47**

# Reference Checking

This is the job that everyone wants to put off until the end or, even better, leave to someone else. I don't know why. It only takes a quick phone call or email. And yet sometimes it gets left right up until the last moment, right before the offer is extended.

Sometimes recruiters don't even check the references themselves and leave it to the employer!

I think the *logic* here is that, if the employer doesn't make an offer to the candidate, then the references are redundant. So why spend time on it?

Why on God's green earth would you spend time marketing a candidate without truly knowing who you're dealing with? Checking references protects your time and the employer from any surprises down the line. It's about getting the real story, not just what's on a resume.

I wonder sometimes if there's a subconscious thing going on here in which recruiters would rather not know if there's something wrong, and they hope that everything just works out. That's understandable to a point. When you've got an amazing candidate, the last thing you want to do is check references and discover a whole closet full of skeletons.

But you have to do it. Because, like it or not, even the most friendly, decent-sounding person is perfectly capable of embellishing, withholding some details, or even flat-out lying. And if there's some bad news to be found, *you* want to be the one who finds it. What do you think it'll do to your credibility when an employer runs the reference and discovers that the candidate you said was purer than the driven snow has a reputation for bullying junior staff?

There's also a clear upside to doing your due diligence. When you present to an employer, it hits differently when you can say, "I checked this person's references, and their supervisor had nothing but good things to say about them." Now, it's not you doing the selling, it's the reference. And that speaks way louder than any opinion you can offer, because it's coming from a neutral party.

It also makes you look more professional. If most recruiters don't do something that is obviously useful to the process, then it's an easy way to set yourself apart.

## How to Conduct a Reference Check

This isn't rocket science. It shouldn't take you more than ten or fifteen minutes. If it does, you're asking the wrong questions. Secondly, this isn't a rubber-stamping exercise; this is an opportunity to uncover golden nuggets that will help you place the candidate or potential problems that you need to know about. It's always more powerful when you can say to an employer that "so-and-so from Company XYZ said that your candidate is one of the sharpest people they ever hired" than it is to simply offer your own opinion.

The only other thing I would say is you don't need to engage your selling powers for this one. If your candidate has given you a good reference, the person on the other end is probably eager to call you and say nice things. In fact, if they don't return your calls or emails, this can be a red flag in itself. Is there a reason why the reference doesn't want to speak with you?

But when you do get on that call, just go through the basics:

- The professional relationship with the candidate

- Their professional competency and aptitude in their field

- Their communication skills and how they work with others

- Confirmation of their work history

- Their eligibility for rehire (if they say: *Absolutely, we'd have them back in a heartbeat,* that's a good sign; but if they say: *No way; never gonna happen,* that's equally helpful . . . just not for the candidate)

- Their strengths and weaknesses

- Their belief in the candidate's ability to perform the position they're applying for

- Any red flags or pertinent details the reference feels you should know about

There's one additional question I like to throw in at the end:

*Is there anything narrative you'd like to add about the candidate?*

This open-ended question can uncover nuances you wouldn't get from a simple yes/no question. Listen carefully to the response, and if you get a hunch that there's something important not being said, be direct and ask them to be straight with you. This is especially useful if the reference is giving you quite bland comments. Use this question to try to get them to go off-script and share how they really feel. You want to make sure there are no surprises further down the line. It's not unheard of for the reference to say one thing to you and something different to the employer. That won't happen if you gently press the reference to be honest and forthcoming.

## Mr. Bad News

I once did a reference check on a guy and was advised that he'd been fired from his former position for cheating on his expense account!

Now, you might be wondering why the candidate would give me a reference for a job where he was fired for fraud. Because I wondered the same thing.

Well . . .

I don't know. There are just some strange fish out there. Maybe he was banking on no one checking the reference. Hard to say. But the candidate, fair play to him, didn't deny it when I put this to him.

*Oh, yeah, I knew that was going to come up.*

What do you do in this scenario? Do you drop him like a hot potato? Sort of. You don't really have much of a choice. You can't try to place a candidate with an employer knowing that he has fraud in his history. But you can at least be straight with them. There's no need to be judgmental.

*Sorry, buddy, but I can't help you. You've got baggage. My advice to you, as your recruiter, is to stay put. If you have an employer who likes you, and you've learned your lesson, stay there. Don't move. You've overcome that objection once with your current employer, but it's going to be incredibly difficult to overcome it again with a new one.*

## Turn References Into Opportunities

If, before you got to this paragraph, you predicted that I was going to tell you to flip the script and try to recruit the references, you're absolutely right.

I know what works, I'm not shy about doing what works, and I'll keep doing what works until they put me out to pasture. If that makes me predictable, then so be it. You could do a lot worse than become a predictable recruiter who takes every opportunity they can.

This is how you put yourself at the top of the tree. A good recruiter's antennae are always tuned in. We think differently from most folks. When I'm talking to anybody, I'm always looking for that market intelligence, that movement. Who's left their company recently? Where did they go? Who have they hired? Was it a tough decision? Were there other candidates they liked?

Obviously, take the reference thoroughly first. Don't scrimp on this part. But afterward, keep the reference talking and see what you can find out.

And if there's nothing immediate to engage with, fall back on that classic close that I'll probably remind you of a few more times yet:

*Look, Ms. Reference, I'm in the market every day, talking to hundreds of people and covering opportunities that are very early in the process and may not even have been publicly announced yet. I would hate to call you sixty or ninety days from now, tell you about a position I just filled (or a candidate I just placed), and have you say, "Gee whiz, Todd, I wish*

> *you'd called me about that." So, if I run into that diamond in the coal mine, that greatest opportunity ever, would you want me to call you?*

Just like that, you've recruited the reference. The next time you call them, they won't know if you want to talk about a candidate or their next dream job. So, they'll *have* to talk to you to find out.

You'll know if you're doing this right and you're genuinely taking every opportunity to recruit, because your database will keep growing, sometimes exponentially. And, best of all, it'll happen organically. Even when you're not getting juice from your cold calls, if you're always recruiting, your business will always be growing.

# Chapter 48

# Nuances of a Contingency Fee Agreement

There's a situation that you'll eventually run into as a recruiter that you won't even have considered until it happens to you.

And it's a stinker!

Imagine you've delivered a great candidate to a client, the employer agrees to hire them, and you're getting ready to deliver the invoice. But then you get a phone call, out of the blue, from another recruiter at another firm. They inform you, in no uncertain terms, that they already sent this candidate's resume to the employer six months earlier, and therefore the fee belongs to them.

Yes, this can and does happen.

The best way to avoid it, of course, is to make sure that you ask the right questions of the employer and the candidate in the first place. If you're digging deep, as you should do, you'll uncover the fact that the candidate has already been presented. Questions such as: *Have you been submitted to any other companies?* and *Have you worked with any other recruiters?* and *Are there any people on a hands-off list I should stay away from?* should reveal any potential conflicts of this type.

But sometimes candidates forget (or they lie), or communication within the employer's workplace isn't the best, and they mess things up. It's not your fault, but now that you're in this pickle, you've got to figure out how to resolve it.

Sometimes you have to accept that another recruiter has a prior claim and concede gracefully. If you've put a lot of work into vetting and prepping the candidate and the other recruiter did nothing more than send a resume over, you could argue for a split of the fee, but if the previous recruiter and the client have a signed agreement, then there's not a lot you can do without getting embroiled in a messy, expensive legal argument that you'll probably lose anyway. Bowing out gracefully and professionally will separate you from your competition in the eye of the employer. Fighting for a split when you're not due one in this instance can damage your reputation and relationship with the employer. It demonstrates professionalism, and that's the impression you want to leave with the employer.

The one thing you must avoid at all costs is a dispute between you and another recruiter impacting the candidate's new position. If the employer gets irritated or anxious about legal action and withdraws the offer, everyone loses. And believe me, the employer and the candidate will tell their friends and colleagues for years about how the "money-grubbing" recruiters ruined their big career move.

Better to take the loss than for that scenario to unfold.

This works the other way around as well. If you present a candidate unsuccessfully to a client but six months later they hire that person after they're presented by another recruiter, you're within your rights to step in and argue that you should be getting some, or even all, of the fee. But again, you don't want to assert this so aggressively that you ruin the deal for the candidate.

It's a fine line. You shouldn't accept being taken advantage of and word getting around that you're a soft touch. But, equally, the priority should be ensuring the candidate doesn't suffer.

Whichever way things unfold, the eventual outcome is likely to hinge on the contingency fee agreement you have with the client. Which is why it's so important that it be clear and watertight. If you're working for a recruitment firm, the agreement you ask the employer to sign has probably been drawn up by lawyers, and making adjustments will be out of your control. But you should still read it carefully and make sure you know exactly what the terms are so you can be aware when another party breaches them.

And if you see something in the agreement that you think could come back to bite you, you're well within your rights to bring it to the attention of your direct report.

Most of the agreement will be in dense legalese, but here are the three main elements to look for:

## 1. The Ownership Period

This describes the length of time after presenting a candidate that the recruiter "owns" the referral. Twelve months is typical, which means that if you present a candidate and the client rejects them, but six months later changes their mind, you are still owed a fee.

It doesn't happen often, but it does happen. Sometimes it's just a communication error, but sometimes unscrupulous employers will delay making an offer to a candidate to try to avoid paying your fee. Don't put up with that nonsense.

A well-defined agreement will also specify precisely when the ownership period starts, such as, for example, when you get an email from the client acknowledging receipt of the candidate's details or, if the candidate was interviewed, the date of the most recent communication with the employer about said candidate. That email is usually admissible in court and indicates when the clock started.

You may also see language around when your candidate is rejected, but you present them again for a different role with the same client or invite the client to take a second look. If the client is amenable to looking at the candidate again, then the agreement will usually clarify that this restarts the clock.

## 2. The Guarantee

The days of offering refunds for placements that fail are gone. Today it's more common for a recruiter to offer some form of "free replacement" guarantee. For example, you could make a placement, but before the candidate can start they unfortunately get sick and can't take up the position. This doesn't happen often, but employers expect recruiters to provide some sort of guarantee in this situation.

The element to focus on is the length of the guarantee. The longer the "free replacement" period, the safer and more secure the client will feel in taking on a candidate, but the more risk the recruiter is taking on.

In my view, thirty days is a reasonable period. I'm not involved in the employer's long-term management of the candidate or any other internal business decisions that might affect the role. We don't insure the candidate, and thirty days is long enough for an employer to determine whether the newly hired employee can perform the requisite work to the satisfaction of the employer. So, as previously discussed (see Chapter Twenty-Five), if the employer wants a longer guarantee, I usually propose that this can be provided in exchange for an additional 1.5 percent increase in our fee for every additional thirty days they require.

One final thing to consider: If it's within your power, you might consider extending a little grace to the employer when something goes wrong, especially if they're a valued client. For instance, if the guarantee period is sixty days, and the candidate unexpectedly quits after sixty-five days, you might still agree to replace the candidate without charge to keep the client satisfied.

## 3. The Fee

The fee is also a critical part of the agreement because it's rarely as simple as calculating 30 percent of a candidate's salary. Bonuses and perks may also need to be factored in if they're significant. Imagine a salesperson who is working for a base salary of $50,000 but is regularly expected to earn $200,000 in a year in commissions. Most recruiters in the sales space expect their fee to be based on total anticipated earnings and not just the base salary.

If you're working for a recruitment firm where the contingency fee agreement is already set, you should at the very least read it through and make sure you're clear on what you're agreeing to when you get a client to sign up. If, however, you're an independent recruiter, I strongly advise you to have your agreement created by qualified legal professionals who, ideally, have plenty of experience with recruitment and understand the kinds of nuances we've discussed here.

# Chapter 49

# Your Recommendations

I was at an event in Málaga, Spain, a couple of years back, and a representative at LinkedIn delivered a talk. The bit I remember most was that 70 percent of businesspeople in the United States are on LinkedIn!

As of April 2025, there are 234 million U.S.-based LinkedIn accounts, but only 171 million civilian workers. You can have a LinkedIn account and be in noncivilian work, or even retired, but that still suggests there are a considerable number of either duplicate accounts or people from overseas pretending to be U.S.-based. Just something to keep in mind. Globally, there are well over a billion LinkedIn members, so it's no surprise that recruiters are heavily dependent on the platform for finding clients and candidates and researching markets. You don't need me to tell you that LinkedIn is a useful tool; you're already using it every day.

But are you fully utilizing it? For example, are you taking advantage of LinkedIn's ability to add Recommendations to your profile page?

Asking clients and candidates for a testimonial or endorsement after a successful placement may be part of your required routine so that your recruitment firm can generate PR material. But what about your personal efforts?

Like it or not, the chances are good that you'll work for more than one recruitment firm during your career. You may even strike out on your own someday. The recommendations for the firm you work for won't follow you to the next stage of your career, but the recommendations on your LinkedIn profile are yours forever.

It's so easy to do. Scroll down on your LinkedIn Profile page to the Recommendations section, hit the + icon, and select Ask for a Recommendation. Repeat this process for everyone at the employer that you interacted with and, of course, the candidate as well. Not everyone will respond, but if you do this after every placement, it won't be long before you're swimming in glowing recommendations.

## Enhanced Reference Checks

Another practical use of recommendations is to enhance the reference check stage (see Chapter Forty-Seven). It's no big secret that candidates select their references because they know they have, or at least have had, a good relationship with them and are likely to say good things. But what happens when we speak to people who know the candidate but aren't on the reference list?

It only takes a little digging on LinkedIn to find people who previously worked with the candidate, and then only a couple of phone calls to find someone who's willing to provide an informal reference.

There are two potential outcomes to this, and both are desirable:

1. If the candidate's previous colleague says nice things, you can present these to the client, emphasizing that this is a recommendation from someone *not* on the reference list. This drives home how desirable the candidate really is.

2. And then on the flip side, if the person tells you something unpleasant about the candidate that they were trying to cover up, it's unfortunate, but better to know than to be in the dark.

# Chapter 50

# Elements of Closing the Deal

The candidate and the employer are in love, and all that's left to figure out is the contract. You're only a step away from a confirmed placement, a happy client, a happy candidate, and a tidy commission.

What could go wrong?

This isn't the time to get nervous. The hard work has already been done, and this final step is often straightforward—you just need to avoid being complacent. That's how you get sloppy and a detail gets missed.

And when things do, unfortunately, fall apart at this late stage, it's almost always due to a small detail you overlooked. You've invested a metric ton of hours into this deal, so don't blow it now by cutting corners and counting the commission dollars before everyone's signed on the dotted line.

Base salary and commission will usually be already settled at this point, unless one side gets greedy and tries a late-stage negotiation. A lot of smaller details might seem insignificant to you, but they could be deal-breaking for the candidate.

Here are some of the details you need to ask about that many recruiters will overlook:

- *Employee Benefits:* This is the most obvious one, but don't be satisfied with the surface-level details. If medical coverage, for example, is included, are there any exclusions? Does it include long-term disability and long-term care? Are co-payments required? What are the premiums? Does the employer pay some or all of the cost of medical coverage?

- *Paid Time Off:* What are the company's policies on vacation time and sick time? Then dig deeper. If the candidate needs a couple of hours off to visit the dentist, does that have to be taken out of vacation time, or can the time be made up later?

- *Business Expenses:* If business expenses are relevant to the position, what's the limit and what is acceptable? How is reporting handled? Manually or digitally? Weekly or monthly? Is it a short form or is the candidate going to be spending two hours a week on business expense paperwork? If a company car is included, who pays the insurance and the gas?

- *Work Location and Amenities:* What is the company's "work from home" policy? Does all the work have to be done from a single office or are there multiple locations? What is the office space like? What kind of perks are provided? Free cafeteria? Free onsite daycare? Free parking?

Why do we need to get this granular? Because if any of these are different from what the candidate is experiencing with their current employer, it can significantly help or hinder the closing of the deal.

If, for instance, the candidate gets health coverage with their current employer but won't with the new employer, that could be an extra $12,000 a year the candidate will have to budget for.

That could wipe out a salary increase in one shot.

Alternatively, if the candidate *doesn't* get healthcare with their current employer, but *does* with the new employer, that's $12,000 going right back into their pocket.

That could be a game-changer.

Maybe the candidate is a bit disappointed with the offer because his current office has a free cafeteria and the new office only has a vending machine. He'll likely get over that pretty quickly if you can point out that he'll save $12,000 a year because he's going to be getting free medical insurance.

Of course, none of this works if you don't know what the candidate is already receiving in his current role. You need to ferret out all this information during the information-gathering stage and go into the same level of detail as described above.

That way, when you negotiate with the new employer on the candidate's behalf, you can spot the differences that might be sticking points or, conversely, differences that might have the candidate dancing in the streets.

A successful recruiter covers all of this exhaustively. This is one of those areas that separate the exceptional consultative recruiter from the rest of the field. You've done great work up to now. Keep that level of quality and attention to detail going, and you'll be far less likely to experience the ugly side of closing the deal.

# Chapter 51

# Back Door Hires

A *back door hire* occurs when an employer engages or hires a candidate after we have presented them and then fails to inform us of the placement. Sometimes this is a simple administration error, but it's more often than not an attempt to bypass the fee agreement and deny you the compensation you're due.

We touched on this in Chapter Forty-Three, and if you've followed protocols and a contingency fee agreement was signed, there is no reason to just roll over and take it. None.

When you challenge the employer, you'll know whether it was a legitimate mistake because they'll either immediately apologize and pay up, or they'll come up with a million excuses why it's really your fault.

They'll say the fee agreement wasn't clear. Or the fee was too high. Or there's documentation missing. Or they already knew about the candidate.

None of this matters, as long as:

- You have a signed contract.

- There is evidence that you introduced the candidate to them, such as an email or database entry).

- The hire took place within the Ownership Period.

- The employer doesn't have a leg to stand on.

And if you have to take legal action to get what you're owed, then so be it.

You must always operate on the bedrock principle that nobody else is going to protect your time or your fee. Only you can do that. This is why it's so important to be thorough in documenting your work. Losing a $30,000 commission because you got excited by the project and didn't ensure the agreement was signed is sickening. It should be noted that some states don't require a signature from the buyer on the agreement, but it's a good habit to get into because it covers you in the event of a dispute and supports your position.

In contingency work, we essentially work for free unless a placement is made, and many clients and candidates won't think twice about wasting our valuable time or trying to take advantage of us. A backdoor hire is the ultimate example of this. Be on guard and remain assertive about your rights and the value you bring to the marketplace.

# Chapter 52

# Closes to Save the Recruiter's Time

In Chapter Twenty-Five, I spoke about the two closes I started employing with more frequency in my fifth year as a recruiter that really helped me up my game, which included the Takeaway Close and Sharp Angle Close. Early in my career, I used the Ben Franklin and The Summary Close which had been serving me pretty well in those early years. But those initial closes had left me with gaps.

Here's a description of the four types:

- *The Benjamin Franklin Close:* So-called because this is reportedly how Franklin made decisions, the candidate draws a line down the center of a piece of paper and lists all of the reasons they should move (the positives) and all the reasons they should stay (the negatives). The idea is to let the candidate find the negatives, while you find the positives, and ultimately produce a much longer list of reasons to move.

- *The Summary Close:* Review the employer's position benefits, compensation, and incentives in one big stack to ensure the candidate has a complete understanding of the entire package and feels overwhelmed by the size of the overall offer.

- *The Sharp Angle Close:* Test the candidate or the employer's commitment by exchanging commitments and clearly setting out the stakes. For example, the candidate agrees to send you their updated resume by the end of the day and, if they don't, you'll assume that they're no longer interested in proceeding (see Chapter Twenty-Four).

- *The Takeaway Close:* Any time you sense doubt or hesitancy from the candidate or employer, instead of trying to persuade them, offer to squash the deal. If they fight to get it back, their interest is genuine. If they let you kill it without challenge, they were never that interested in the first place (see Chapter Twenty-Four and many others).

All the above have their uses, but the gaps in the first two was an ability to filter out the people who aren't truly motivated. I recognized this and I decided to double down on the last two. The Sharp Angle Close and the Takeaway Close became the bedrock of my work. I used it in virtually every conversation and negotiation. Even when it might have seemed like I was actively trying to torpedo a deal, I didn't care. I was driven by this idea that if I could weed out all the tire-kickers at the earliest stage, I would only spend my time on the real deals that had a chance for a successful conclusion.

What happened next?

In year five, I broke $200,000 for the first time and the year after I billed $275,000. In two years, I had increased my previous billing peak by over 50 percent.

And the numbers kept growing.

The next year, I breached the $300,000 barrier. Two years later, the $400,000 barrier. Then the $500,000 barrier.

At my peak, I billed a bit over $799,000 with an average fee of $13,000. Did I mention I only worked thirty-nine weeks in my best production year?

And bear in mind, this was in 1999. Adjusting for inflation and the increase of the average fee, today that would be over $1.5 million.

In just one year.

Some of this can be attributed to the steady growth in my network, but I know lots of other recruiters who have grown their network at similar rates to me but haven't billed nearly as much. I attribute my success in this area to ruthlessly employing those last two closes. Rather than wasting time babysitting deals that had no chance to come together, my energies were focused on activities that had a real chance to close.

Did I lose some deals in the process?

Almost certainly. I'm sure I nuked the occasional deal with a Takeaway Close that came too soon and too aggressively. But for every deal I lost through this method, I probably avoided ninety-nine *opportunities* that would have been a waste of time.

I've mentioned the benefits of these closes a few times in this book, but I'm bringing it up one final time and tying it into my overall financial success because I want to drive home how important it is to manage and protect your time.

It's the difference between achieving marginal success and reaching an elite level.

Recruiting is like a giant puzzle, and one of the biggest mistakes a rookie recruiter makes is investing sweat equity into activities that have no chance of coming together. It takes guts to adopt these closes and use them convincingly. But the sooner you try it, the sooner you'll start to see real results.

If I had known all this in my first couple of years as a recruiter, I've no doubt that I would have accelerated my billing figures faster and sooner. So, my challenge to you, especially if you're in the early days of your recruitment career, is to learn those closes cold, and have the courage to use them rigorously.

Do this, and you'll thank me someday.

# The More Things Change the More They Stay the Same

How often do I think about the Roman Empire?

Probably every day.

Think I'm exaggerating? Well, around fifteen years ago, I gave a presentation at a regional meeting for Management Recruiters International (MRI). And I decided to attend dressed in a full suit of Roman centurion armor.

Not a cheap Halloween costume with a foam sword—I mean the full getup. Helmet with a crest, leather sandals, greaves, gladius (sword), pugio (dagger), and a red battle tunic. Most important, the *lorica segmentate*—overlapping iron strips covering the shoulders and torso. I'm six-foot- one, but with the crest of the helmet and the imposing armor, I probably looked closer to seven feet.

I walked into the room and the atmosphere changed. People saw this giant who could have been a stunt double in the *Gladiator* movie, striding across the floor, armor clanking, looking for all the world like someone ready to go into battle.

I picked an anxious-looking recruiter at random, drew my gladius (a short, double-edged sword), and thrust the tip under his chin.

*"Salve amicus es?"* I bellowed.

The poor guy's eyes were huge and the whole room went silent.

I then translated my question for the room and for my relieved victim: *Are you not my friend*?

If you've been paying attention, you'll recognize that this question is a callback to one of my most important questions for a budding recruiter:

> *Do you want to be known as a recruiter, or a friend who happens to be a recruiter?*

This was more than just pageantry. This was a dramatic hook to get their attention and ensure they remembered the evening I got on stage and explained why the bedrock of successful action hasn't changed since the days of the Roman Empire.

Without replaying the entire speech, I outlined a comparison between the Romans' domination of the world, and the same tenets that we must apply as recruiters:

- The Romans didn't enter battle without tremendous military *preparation*—so too we cannot have an effective day with making a plan for who we're going to call and what we're going to say.

- Roman legions learned absolute *discipline* so they could hold their ground when the barbarians charged—so too we need discipline to stick to our daily schedule and not bounce between calls, emails, and LinkedIn.

- The Romans rotated their front lines, using a centurion's signal to *execute* a practiced switch to fresh troops—so too we must plan and practice our questions so that when someone finally answers the phone we can execute flawlessly and gather every piece of valuable information.

- Much of the time, the Romans earned their success through overwhelming *numbers*—so too we achieve victory through the sheer number of calls and conversations that we carry out every day.

The more things change, the more they stay the same, indeed.

For us, there's an even more relevant parallel: Though technology has developed rapidly in recent decades and is now progressing faster than ever, the principles of good recruitment are still the same.

I wouldn't go back to using the yellow pages to find numbers, and five-by-seven cards to make call notes. LinkedIn and databases make it possible to be more targeted with our conversations and make it easier and faster to record the details. But the underlying principle of talking to people and building connections is the same, so the technology helps rather than hinders.

This isn't true of all technology. We're at the point where AI can write a job advert, candidates can set their AI to automatically send a resume, and then AI will review the incoming applications. That might be okay (maybe—the jury's still out on this one) for entry-level positions where hiring is being done at scale, but this is not conducive to building relationships.

It doesn't matter how many time-saving and labor-saving devices recruiters are gifted, they must not, and cannot, replace the human element. You cannot establish a relationship of trust via email, direct message, or AI. Ultimately, you have to talk to people.

You will never get inside a person's head and truly understand their motivation, their hopes, dreams, and desires without a real conversation.

This is why executive recruiters are indispensable and irreplaceable. We are problem-solvers, delivering a solution to both the client and the candidate. We are matchmakers, aligning the candidate's hopes, dreams, and desires with the client's needs. Any fool can learn how to use the latest software and apps. But it takes a smart recruiter to recognize how the tech will enhance their conversations with candidates and clients, rather than trying to delegate away the most important part of their skillset.

When I took over as the owner of my recruitment business, taking care of a team of twenty-two employees, one of the recruiters who had been around for a long time began telling everyone not to listen to me and that "The old man has lost it. He's a dinosaur."

First of all, I was in my fifties—that's not even close to being old—and secondly, I'd worked a recruitment desk for eighteen years and outperformed everybody for much of that time. And just because I'd moved into management, I was out of touch? I wasn't some greenhorn executive, parachuted in to take over a business I knew nothing about. I'd done my time on the floor, and I'd excelled.

Fortunately, news about the slander got back to me. I could have just fired the individual, and I certainly would have had grounds. But then to everyone else, it might look like what he'd been saying was true and that I was afraid of him.

Ha!

Instead, I took my anger and channeled it into action. There was an empty desk out in the bullpen, so I sat down and began making calls. Within six weeks, I placed a candidate on a $300,000 salary and earned a $90,000 commission. I did this in full view and earshot of everyone. They even got to hear one of those classic conversations where HR balked at the invoice because the role was filled so quickly and I stuck to my guns and got the full fee.

People around me were throwing down their headsets, gobsmacked that after a few years in a management role, I could so easily jump back into recruiter mode, in an industry I didn't specialize in, and quickly make a major placement.

Needless to say, no one ever called me a dinosaur again.

My naysayer had spectacularly missed the point. Just because I wasn't hands-on with the latest recruitment technology didn't mean I was over the hill. Because the more technology changes, the more the thing that really matters stays the same.

Relationships are everything. When you operate from a place of friendship and trust, your advice is better received, whether it is by a candidate or a hiring authority. I was always up front and honest, always doing what was best for them, which is why clients kept coming back to me. When you build true partner relationships, your clients trust you at face value, and sometimes those relationships deepen into real friendships.

The short version?

I'd taken to heart the core philosophy of this book:

*It's not about you!*

This is the hill I will gladly die on. It's not about us. We take ourselves out of the equation. It's about solving the client's problem and serving the candidate. Make this the North Star of your work. Your job is simply to match great people with great employers.

You only have one reputation in this business. And if you're always careful to do the right thing by the people you serve, regardless of what that might mean for your commission in any given situation, you'll eventually have the kind of recruitment career you've always dreamed of.

# Acknowledgments

I want to give heartfelt thanks to Gary Adams for the daily recruiter training, guidance, and advice he provided during the first half of my recruiting career. He was my greatest mentor to whom I owe so much.

I'm also very grateful and want to recognize Brian Doherty, Jack Downing, and Gary Fruchtman for their tutelage and unwavering support when I first became and continued on as a recruiting firm owner.

I'd like to give a shout out to Dave Sanders whose direction and encouragement was the impetus to write this book so other recruiting professionals would be able to learn from my experience.

Last and certainly not least, I want to thank David C for his guidance completing this project.

# About the Author

Todd Dawson has been with MRI/WorldBridge Partners Omaha since 1985 and became the President in 2002. As one of the founding members of WorldBridge Partners, he oversees the most tenured office in WorldBridge with three separate business practices, including Banking and Financial Services, Insurance, and Legal.

Todd directs the WBP National Insurance and Legal Practices. Omaha's team consists of twelve consultants with over 140 years of experience partnering and providing clients with solutions to their pressing talent acquisition and hiring process needs. With over six thousand professionals placed since 1968, WBP Omaha has billed over $165 million in client services.

Todd has over forty years of successful consulting experience and while on a solo desk, had personally accounted for over $8 million in billed services. Todd was recognized seven times as the Midwest Regional Account Executive of the Year and named the Solo Account Executive of the Decade for the 1990s for Management Recruiters International. He was inducted into the exclusive MRI Summit Club in 1990, of which there are only fourteen members in all of MRI's search professionals. Todd earned his CSAM (Certified Senior Account Manager) status in 1987 and was CSAM of the year in 1997. He was inducted into the MRI Hall of Fame in 1991, gained the Ring of Honor in 2010, and was awarded his MRI Lifetime Achievement Award in 2017.

Todd earned his Bachelor of Science in Criminal Justice from the University of Nebraska at Omaha in 1977 and spent seven years in law enforcement prior to becoming a search consultant. Todd is married with three sons and enjoys sports and traveling the world.